THE GIFT
OF
CHURCH

HOW GOD DESIGNED the LOCAL CHURCH
to MEET OUR NEEDS AS CHRISTIANS

THE GIFT
OF
CHURCH

JIM SAMRA

ZONDERVAN®

ZONDERVAN.com/
AUTHORTRACKER
follow your favorite authors

We want to hear from you. Please send your comments about this book to us in care of zreview@zondervan.com. Thank you.

ZONDERVAN

The Gift of Church
Copyright © 2010 by James G. Samra

This title is also available as a Zondervan ebook. Visit www.zondervan.com/ebooks.

This title is also available in a Zondervan audio edition. Visit www.zondervan.fm.

Requests for information should be addressed to:
Zondervan, *Grand Rapids, Michigan 49530*

Library of Congress Cataloging-in-Publication Data

Samra, James George
    The gift of church : how God designed the local church to meet our needs as Christians / Jim Samra.
      p. cm.
      ISBN 978-0-310-29309-5 (softcover)
      1. Parishes. 2. Church. I. Title.
    BV700.S15 2010
    250—dc22   2010019076

Cover design: Tammy Johnson
Cover photography: Trevillion Images
Interior design: Sherri L. Hoffman

Printed in the United States of America

---

10 11 12 13 14 15 /DCI/ 21 20 19 18 17 16 15 14 13 12 11 10 9 8 7 6 5 4 3 2 1

*To Calvary, along with all other churches
who are striving to be the amazing gift that
God has designed them to be*

CONTENTS

ACKNOWLEDGMENTS

I am grateful first and foremost to the Lord Jesus Christ, who loved me and gave himself for me. Thank you, Jesus, for giving to us the gift of church. We are sorry for the ways that we have failed to be the church, but we are grateful for your continued presence with us wherever two or three gather in your name. Everything good about this book has come from you. You have guided the entire process from start to finish and have been faithful in every possible way.

I would like to express appreciation to those churches who have loved and shaped my family and me. For Northeast Bible Church (Garland, Texas) and Calvary Baptist Church (Grand Rapids, Michigan), respectively, where Lisa and I became Christians as young children and learned to love Jesus. For Fellowship Bible Church (Ann Arbor, Michigan) and Grace Covenant Church (Austin, Texas), where we each found the presence of God in the midst of secular college campuses. For Oak Cliff Bible Fellowship (Oak Cliff, Texas) and Lake Ridge Bible Church (Mesquite, Texas), where we were ministered to and learned to minister while in seminary. For St. Andrews (Oxford, England), where we learned that even when you cross an ocean, God is present in and through his church. And especially for Calvary Church (Grand Rapids, MI), where our entire family has experienced what it means to truly be part of God's church. Each church was the true manifestation of the body of Christ for us.

I am incredibly appreciative to the pastoral staff at Calvary Church, who willingly interacted with me and this material for many years. It is a distinct pleasure to serve God with you, and the ideas in this book are much better because we are trying to live them out in real life. I am grateful to the elders and deacons of Calvary Church, who have been incredibly supportive, and to the entire church family, who has loved us unconditionally.

I am daily thankful for my sweet wife, who has read this manuscript countless times and is an incredible editor in her own right. More than that, she is my best friend and an amazing co-laborer in ministry. I have the opportunity to put these ideas into practice every day with her as my partner in ministry, and it is a great joy. I am grateful to my beautiful children for being such an amazing source of joy in my life. I am also thankful for my parents, who first taught me to love the church.

I am grateful to the people at Zondervan who helped make this project a reality. For Stan Gundry and Paul Engle, who helped conceive this idea and bring it to fruition. For Ryan Pazdur, who demonstrated great editorial abilities and was a pleasure to work with. For Chris Fann and his marketing and promotion team for their ideas and support. For Verlyn Verbrugge, who provided insightful comments as a preacher and an insightful editor.

Finally, I am grateful to all those who have seen the beauty of the church and daily strive to make it a place of grace, hope, and love in their communities. Thank you for all that you do.

INTRODUCTION

I recently received an email from a woman describing her church history to me. She had been in a wide range of churches — some were judgmental, some internally focused, one rather cold and unwelcoming, another unappreciative of her service, and still another weak theologically. She had visited every church within a fifty-mile radius of her home. Unable to find one that she thought was suitable, she wrote to me because she was listening to podcasts of my sermons. In her email she asked, "Is listening to sermons at home alone enough, or do I still need to go to church?"

I know a couple with three young children. They are typical parents who want their children to excel. The children are involved in dance programs, sports, preschool, play dates, and much more. All this activity doesn't leave much time or energy to be involved in a local church. The parents host a weekly Bible study in their home that provides some teaching and Christian fellowship. The parents are convinced that this is all they and their children need. Are they right?

Mason is a successful businessman.[1] He is sure that if he ran his business the way most churches are run, he would be bankrupt within a few weeks. Consequently, he has little time or respect for the church. He and some likeminded businessmen will often invite teachers to come and address their group, or just get together for accountability and mutual encouragement. He feels closer to these men than to his own brothers. For him, this group is his "church," and he doesn't need any other. Is there any reason for him to become involved in a local church?

A friend of mine who teaches at a Christian college recently told me that roughly 70 percent of the student population are not regularly engaged in a local church. Between mandatory chapel services, easy fellowship with other students, missions and service opportunities through the school, and busy schedules, most students find church to be redundant. Are they right?

A study in Britain covering 1990–2000 found that during this time, weekly church attendance dropped from 28 percent to 8 percent, while the number of people reporting spiritual experiences rose from 48 percent to 76 percent. In the United States, 60 percent believe that churches are unnecessary, because we have God within us.[2] Is church unnecessary?

I have spent a long time wrestling with these questions. Except for the times when I had an illness (whether actual or feigned), I attended church every Sunday with my family as a child and young adult. But I never really understood why we went. Sometimes it was an unpleasant experience, and I would ask, "Why bother with church?" Hebrews 10:25 was quoted to me: "Let us not give up meeting together, as some are in the habit of doing." But this was not convincing. One verse—that's it? If that's the theological reason for going to church, why can't I just meet with other Christians? Do I have to attend an actual service?

Others told me: "It's where we learn about God; it's where you grow as a follower of Jesus." But I figured that I could learn about God just as well from my family, from reading books, from watching television (and now the Internet), or through school.

Still others just appealed to tradition and habit: "That's what Christians have always done." While I'm not one to ignore tradition, it seemed at the time just a way of deflecting the question. So, I repeat, why should we go to church?

One publication I read listed the question, "Why do I have to go to church?" as the first of seven tough questions that children ask about life and faith and suggested that when asked this question, parents might try responding like this: "Families do certain things together and this is something our family does together. Our family goes to family reunions at Grammy's house. We cheer for each other on the ball field. We support each other when we are having a hard time. And we worship in church together."[3] That may convince a seven-year-old, but is "family bonding" really the primary reason we should participate in church?

This question — "Why church?" — continued to plague me as I grew older. Even as God was calling me into ministry and sending me to a local church to work, I was unable to articulate why people needed to be involved with the church — a rather awkward position to be in. But God was gracious to me and began answering my question — in part through three years of doctoral research spent trying to find an answer. This book is my attempt to share some of those answers with you and with others who may have similar questions.

THE BEST ARGUMENT AGAINST CHURCH

Let's begin by acknowledging up front the single best argument *against* the church, namely, the church itself. No other group of people falls so far short of what it is meant to be. Martin Luther said it well: "There is no greater sinner than the Christian church."[4]

When I was in junior high, I was labeled one of the "bad kids" by my church. When our youth group would meet together, I was allowed to join the main group, but when we broke up into small groups I was assigned to a group by myself. No other students. No leaders. After I'd been there awhile, others who had been kicked out of their groups joined me in my exile — we became the Australia of junior high small groups. Eventually there were enough of us in the problem group that a leader was assigned to us, but he spent most of our time together reminding us how much trouble we were causing. My primary faults were talking too much and disrupting the class. I also went to movies, listened to secular music, and did not attend Christian schools. When I applied to go on a short-term mission trip with the church, I was told that I was not "spiritual" enough to go. When I asked the leaders how I could become *more* spiritual, I was told that I needed to go on a short-term mission trip! In frustration, I asked for some help from the youth pastor, but he told me that he had no time for me. Eventually, I discovered that the only way I would lose the label of being a "bad kid" was for our family to switch to another church. I recognize that others have certainly had far worse experiences with the church, but for me this was still rather difficult. I felt a keen sense of rejection and suffered haunting doubts about my own salvation and acceptance by God.

If you've spent any time in different churches, you can likely attest to the sad truth that sinful attitudes and prejudices continue to exist in many of our churches. Once, I attended a church service where the senior pastor stood up at the end of a solo musical performance and began to verbally criticize the shy cellist because he felt that she had not done a very good job. I know of another church that would actually turn away visitors who were not dressed to their legalistic standards. Yet another church advised a pastor's wife to continue allowing her husband to physically abuse her for the sake of unity and the witness of the church in the community. One guest preacher at a church delivered a sermon that was so filled with racist propaganda that the senior pastor had to actually stand up and rebuke his guest and chastise his own congregation for applauding.

I know of a church that divided because some of the members were involved in sexually immoral behavior, and they were not happy when they were told that this was unbiblical. Even worse, this included some of the leaders on the pastoral staff! Another church fired one of their pastors because one of the wealthier members of the church didn't like him, and they threatened to quit giving if he was not removed from his position. Still another church paid their senior pastor an extravagant sum of money, while ignoring the needs of the poor in their community. I've seen a church ask a family with a special needs child to stop coming to church because the child made others uncomfortable.

These are just a small sample of the ugliness that we find in the Christian church. And these are just churches I have been involved with or been made aware of—this doesn't even *begin* to scratch the surface! If you've been involved with the church for very long, you probably have your own stories to tell. The sad truth is that the church has been a legalistic, hypocritical, immoral, blasphemous, abusive, dictatorial, selfish, vindictive, uncommitted, disbelieving, judgmental, introspective, mean-spirited, proud, manipulative institution. And worst of all has been these things while claiming to represent God.

Nor should we assume that this is a recent development. In the New Testament, we read about a church, two thousand years ago in the city of Corinth (present-day Greece), that embraced the cult of personality and, on the basis of personal allegiance, had divided into competing factions. The church had a member who was sleeping with his father's wife, with the approval of the majority of churchgoers! Christians were taking other Christians to court, some Christians were sleeping with prostitutes, and the wealthier believers in the church were refusing to share their food with the poor believers during the community meals. Worship services were a disorderly competition to see who was more gifted, and some in the church denied a basic belief of the faith, saying that there was no resurrection of the dead.

The best argument *against* the church has always been the church itself.

THE BEST ARGUMENT FOR THE CHURCH

So how do we respond to this list of charges? What can we say when faced with the mess and the failure of this sacred institution? Why would anyone actually want to go to church? Why would anyone want to participate in a church or recommend a church to another person? Rather than try to defend the church or offer excuses for its failures,[5] I'd like to suggest there is one argument for the church that trumps all the failures of the church — if we are ready to believe it. It's the idea that *God designed and created the church for our benefit and for his glory.*

We must never forget that *God created the church.* It's his idea! Jesus said, "I will build *my* church" (Matt. 16:18). He is the architect and the builder of church. The church in the book of Acts is presented as the work of the Holy Spirit, a creation of God built in accordance with the plan of Jesus. The church is not the invention of the disciples of Jesus. Those who participate in church participate in an entity whose architect and builder is God. Paul wrote "to the church *of God* in Corinth" (1 Cor. 1:2). He addressed his letter this way because the church is the collection of people who have God as their source and object. The church is God's field, God's building, God's temple, the family of God, the body of Christ, the bride of Christ, and the fellowship of the Spirit. Social historians can describe its formation and recognize its sociological distinctives. Biblical historians can acknowledge the role that the apostles had in founding and instructing churches. But the Bible clearly teaches that God designed the church; he is still building it today; and he has given it to us as a gift for our benefit and his glory.

This truth gives the church an inherent, inviolable value. Before we pass judgment on the church because of the obvious moral failures and the apparent sin, we also need to remember that the church shares the same problem that any human institution faces: you and me. Our fallen, sinful nature just happens to be more noticeable in the church because the church is where "you" and "I" become "we" — and when we try to work together, our failures are magnified and compounded.

Despite our failures, human beings have value because we are created by God in his image. And as Christians, we are also being *re-created* by God in the image of Christ. In the church our multiplied failures meet his infinite grace and power. At the end of the day, the fact that God created the church for us is the best argument for why believing Christians should involve themselves in a local body of believers. This is not an excuse to minimize or ignore the failures we find in the church, nor is it meant to pass over the very real problems the church faces. All over, we find churches where God's original design has been abused, gutted, and changed from the amazing gift he intended for his people.

Nevertheless, despite the fact that churches have deviated from God's intention, the value of the church is found in recognizing that it is God's idea, the product of his creative design and the recipient of his empowering Spirit. We love the church because it is a gift from God. We participate in the church because God does. We do not give up on the church, because God refuses to.

In spite of its manifold failures, God's church has been the means by which people throughout history and across the world have experienced true love, acceptance, grace, and forgiveness. Through the church, people have come to know Jesus and by his grace have grown to be more like him. Churches have fed the poor, healed the sick, and overcome the powers of darkness. They have spoken the truth about Jesus to the world and loved God and their neighbors as well.

BENEFITS OF CHURCH

Now I don't expect you to become a fan of the church just yet. When I claim that God created the church for our benefit and his glory, and that it is really a gift to us — for our good and for his name — this should naturally raise a question in your mind: *In what way does the church benefit us?* This book seeks to answer that question. My goal is not to promote a certain model of church. I am not trying to tell you how to do church or the best way to set up a worship service or to reach your community. Instead, I am writing to answer just one, simple question:

What benefit is the church?[6]

You may very well be saying to yourself: "I've never received *any* benefits from being involved in the church. The church has only caused me pain—and many churches seem to have done damage to the witness of Christ in this world." Unfortunately, this is all too common, but this book would be pointless if I (and millions of others throughout history) hadn't had incredibly powerful experiences of the church being what God designed and intended it to be. Still, I have met people who have not had those experiences, and that may be true for you as well. Right now, you may be in a situation where the failures of the church are just too much to bear.

Before you give up on the church altogether (or if you have already given up on the church), I want you to consider one possibility. Is it the *design* of the church that is fundamentally flawed? Or is the design of the church good, but just badly implemented? My hope is that you'll continue reading and give me an opportunity to show how God's design for the church, despite bad implementation at times, is still an amazing gift to his people and to the world. Will you take a few moments to join me in exploring the beauty of his creation?

GOING FORWARD

Let's begin by defining what the church is and is not. This raises a number of questions and possible distinctions that we need to make. For example, what is the difference between a church and a parachurch (an organization that takes on certain functions of a church, but generally not all of them)? To what extent is the church a *human* institution and to what extent is it a *divine* organism? When we talk about the church, are we talking about the group down the street (the local church) or the people of God throughout history, from every nation on earth (the universal church)?

We don't have time to dive deeply into all of these questions. Still, we need some sort of working framework from which to proceed. Let me suggest that we define a church, as we discuss it in this book, as a regular gathering of at least two or three people assembled in the name of Lord Jesus Christ. This is the basic definition of the church derived from Matthew 18:20. Expanding this further, I would argue that to be a church such a group should be committed to the following:

1. doing the whole mission of God
2. preaching the Word and rightly administering the sacraments
3. confessing sin and exercising church discipline
4. basing membership on Christ alone
5. covenanting together
6. being united
7. leading pastorally
8. operating in grace

Let me also say that when I talk about church in this book, I am for the most part talking about the local church. The Bible uses the exact same word for both the local church and the universal church. This indicates a close connection between the two. The easiest way to say this is that the universal church is available to us in and through the local church.

Therefore, following the pattern of the Bible, this book uses "church" with a lowercase "c," usually indicating the local church, sometimes referring to the universal church, and sometimes indicating both. A fuller discussion of what these different aspects of the church mean and several related questions are included in the appendix at the end of the book, but much of what we've defined here will become clear as we look more closely at how God designed the church for our benefit.

The following chapters unfold some of the richness of how God has designed church for our benefit, and the points laid out are cumulative. In chapter 1, I argue that the most basic benefit of the church is that it is the means by which we experience the tangible presence of God in this world today. Nowhere is God as present as he is in the midst of his gathered church.

Chapter 2 builds on this point by arguing that because the church is where God is uniquely present, church is the means by which God redeems our diversity as he draws all men and women to himself in unity. When diverse human beings come together in Jesus, true community is formed.

Chapter 3 examines why the church is the place where we find the City of God today, and how it is the means by which we *experience* this true community.

Chapter 4 looks at how we become spiritually mature as God unifies us in Christ as a diverse people. This happens in the church in a way that cannot happen in other institutions.

Chapter 5 argues that this growing body of the church is able to accomplish, qualitatively and quantitatively, more than any other collection of humans can accomplish.

Finally, chapter 6, building on the others, demonstrates that church is the means by which the invisible Jesus is made visible for us—and the world—to see.

I would like to add one more element in describing this book—that it is a book of *ideas*. It is a book about God's design. It is *not* a book of *practice*. Hopefully, reading this book will raise hundreds of questions in your mind. Perhaps it will raise some objections, and there will likely be many disagreements about how all of this works out on a practical level. Thankfully, there are many books available that spell out the practical ways that we can be the church. At our church, we are doing our best, by the grace of God, to put these truths into practice. Other churches are trying to do this as well. But let's not make the mistake of trying to make the church into something it was never designed to be. Understanding the design of the church frees us to let the church be what it was intended to be.

THE TWO-THOUSAND-YEAR-OLD REVOLUTION

Recognizing that the church is a gift from God designed for our benefit and his glory is a journey that all of us have to take at some point in our Christian lives if we are going to be fully engaged with the plans and purposes of God in Christ. As we prepare to embark on this journey in the following chapters, let me share with you the experience of one fellow traveler. In 2006 Peter Furler, the lead singer for the band Newsboys, said in an interview that for about fifteen years he had "left the church"— by which he meant, "We didn't have a connection or a home base. We didn't have pastors and leaders in our lives. We just were a group of nomads who roamed the earth."

> When asked how he stayed strong during that period of wandering, Peter replied, "I didn't. I really didn't. That's probably why I'm back in church and why I believe in wise counseling—having men around you that you want to be like. For me, it wasn't so much in some big moral failure. It was more a failure of the heart. Where there is no hope, your heart sort of starts to void. As I got older, I questioned not so much Jesus, but the plans and purposes of God. There's been a lot of talk about *purpose* in the past few years, but I began to realize I can't really enter into my purpose until I understand what God is doing. I started to get a real kingdom revelation; I realized there was a revolution that started a couple thousand years ago. Jesus died and he's building a kingdom, and it's the only hope that racism, poverty, and all afflictions on earth are going to disappear. That began to thrill me and it began to change our music a little." As God called Peter to lead people in true worship, he came back into church to get aligned with the plans and purposes of God for himself and for this world.[7]

My prayer for you is that like Peter, you will discover the value of the church as a gift from God to us.

CHAPTER 1

GOD IN CONCERT

One of the few things original to our house is a nearly one-hundred-year-old Concord grapevine. Soon after we moved in, our family, on a whim, decided to make our own juice from the grapes on the vine. After a little online research, we had a plan. We picked over twenty pounds of grapes, washed them, and then smashed them into a pulpy mess. After boiling the pulp, we added a little sugar and then strained the mixture several times through cheesecloth to filter the juice.

What remained was the most amazing juice I have ever tasted. It was stunningly better than the store-bought grape juice we normally drank. This juice was rich, tangy, and luscious. The taste just exploded in my mouth when I drank it. It felt thick, almost like a fruit smoothie. I savored every sip of it.

While I can use vivid words to describe that juice and spend hours talking about it, the truth is that nothing can compare to actually tasting it. If a picture is worth a thousand words, then a sip of that juice is easily worth a million.

In Psalm 34:8 we are invited to "taste and see that the LORD is good." This is an invitation to you and me to experience God for ourselves. Second Corinthians 3:18 tells us that in some wonderful way, we can behold the Lord's glory. As wonderful as words are for describing and talking about God, nothing can compare to actually experiencing him: seeing him, hearing his voice, or feeling his presence.

When Jesus walked the earth two thousand years ago, the apostle John could truthfully write that he had seen, heard, and touched the Word of life (1 John 1:1 – 3). But how can you and I experience God intimately? Although there are a number of ways available for this, God intends for us to experience his presence in a unique and powerful way *through the church, because God is uniquely present when the church assembles.* In other words, God is "seen," "tasted," and experienced in the midst of the gathered assembly of the church. Let's explore what this means by looking at some passages from the Old and New Testaments related to the gathering of God's people and the presence of God in their midst.

THE BIG DAY!

The theme of God's presence with his people begins in the Old Testament and progresses as we move into the New, with the unfolding of God's plan. When we encounter God in the opening narrative of Exodus, he seems distant and unknown; no one seems to have heard from or seen God for hundreds of years. The only thing the people have, as they struggle through life in Egypt, are the ancient stories of the patriarchs, muddled through generations of retelling. But by the time we reach the end of Exodus, each and every single Israelite, free from the tyranny of Egypt, is regularly experiencing God's tangible presence (Ex. 40:34 – 38) and living in the defining reality of belonging to God as one of his people (33:16).

The turning point in the story that accounts for Israel's enjoying regular, habitual interaction with God is not the burning bush (Ex. 3), nor the ten plagues (Ex. 7 – 11), nor the parting of the Red Sea (Ex. 14). The turning point comes in the middle of the book, with the gathering of a sacred assembly at Mount Sinai (Ex. 19 – 20). There the nation of Israel sees the visible evidence of God's presence as smoke and fire rains down on the mountain and they hear the voice of God speaking directly to them. This was a hair-raising, jaw-dropping, quake-in-your-boots, fall-over-backward experience of God! God spoke directly to the people, making his presence visible and audible, and it became one of the most memorable and significant days in the history of the nation.

One of the great Christian leaders of our era, John Stott, once wrote the following in his diary as a young man, in the days following his conversion to Christianity:

> Yesterday was an eventful day ... up until now Christ has been on the circumference and I have but asked him to guide me instead of giving him complete control ... I really have an immense and new joy throughout the day. It is the joy of being at peace with the world and in touch with God. How well do I know now that he rules me and that I never really knew him before.[8]

As Stott discovered in his own life, there is an important difference between simply being aware of God — that he exists — and actually experiencing his presence. We may know that God is out there somewhere, but the *experience* of God is unforgettable! That was the experience Israel had that day when they met with God on the mountain. It was the beginning of their ongoing relationship with God — a day they would never forget.

Typically on a day of such great importance, we give it a title so that we can easily remember and refer to it. We do this with special days like our birthday or wedding day, or with days of national remembrance like Independence Day, or Black Tuesday, or 9/11. Because the day of God's appearance at Mount Sinai was so significant to Israel's history, it, too, was given a name — a title to commemorate the experience. They didn't call it "The Day of the Appearance" or "Ten Commandments Day" (though either of those would have been accurate). Instead, it was called "the day of the assembly" (see Deut. 9:10; 10:4; 18:16; cf. 4:10). The reason for this specific title was because God wanted to remind Israel that they had experienced his presence *in the midst of their assembly.* The Day of the Assembly forever became a part of the history of God's people, because on that day God not only forged a relationship with Israel, he also established a pattern—they would experience him most fully, not simply as individuals or through mediators, but by gathering together in assembly.

MORE ASSEMBLIES

Moreover, on important days like a wedding, we often want to take aspects of that day with us after the event has passed so that we can reexperience parts of it over and over again. For example, my wife and I intentionally saved a portion of our wedding cake so that we could eat it on our first anniversary. Sadly, when we tried to enjoy this memory a year later, a combination of freezer burn and an unfortunate spill in the car during transportation ensured that all we experienced was the nasty smell of rotting cake for months after our first anniversary! But the intent was to re-create one aspect of that life-changing day.

Because the Day of Assembly was so important, God designed ways for the people to take aspects of their experience on Mount Sinai with them long after that day had passed. As they were preparing to leave Mount Sinai, God gave to Moses instructions for a mobile tent called *the tabernacle*, which would allow him to be present wherever the nation travelled. It was a mobile home for God—God's tent whenever Israel went camping. This mobile dwelling allowed the nation to take that experience on Mount Sinai with them wherever they went. To re-create the event of that day, God commanded that the people, whenever they stopped to set up camp, set his tent in the middle of the camp (Num. 2:2) and then gather the whole nation around him at specific times for sacred assemblies (Lev. 23).

During these assemblies, God promised to be present in their midst once again—much like he had been on Mount Sinai (e.g., Deut 31:9–13). Because God was present at these times, such gatherings were described as being "before the LORD" (e.g., Lev. 9:5; Judg. 20:1–2; 1 Chron. 29:20), and the assembling together of the people became known simply as "the assembly of the LORD" (e.g., Deut. 23:2–8; 1 Chron. 28:8; Mic. 2:5). By assembling together around the tabernacle, God was providing a means for Israel to continue to experience his unique presence as they had at Mount Sinai.

After several years, Israel stopped wandering and settled into more permanent dwellings. Eventually, a more permanent house was built for God, known as *the temple*. The purpose of the temple was similar to that of the tabernacle. The temple and the assemblies that happened there were meant to re-create the foundational experience of God at Mount Sinai. So when the time came to dedicate the temple, all of Israel gathered *in assembly* and God was present in a unique and powerful way once more, filling the temple with his glory (1 Kings 6–8). Like the tabernacle, Israel continued to assemble regularly at the temple and frequently experienced God's visible presence while hearing his voice in a unique way (e.g., 2 Chron. 20; 34:29–31; Ps. 122; Joel 2:12–27).

For Israel, God's unique presence — the kind of presence experienced in a powerful, unprecedented way on Mount Sinai — was permanently linked to their assembling together. It's not that God *wasn't* present in other places or active at other times. It's just that he was more *fully* and *tangibly* present when the people of God assembled together.

AN UNFORTUNATE LINGUISTIC TWIST OF FATE

We know this was true for the nation of Israel, but that was a long time ago. What about us today? Where do we go if we want to experience God in a powerful and unique way? Where is our Mount Sinai, our tabernacle ... our temple? For those reading the Bible in Greek, the answer is more readily obvious. Sadly, English speakers are the victims of an unfortunate linguistic twist of fate. The key word we have examined so far has been the word we translate "assembly." In Hebrew, this word is *qahal*, and at the time of the New Testament, this Hebrew word was regularly translated into the Greek language as *ekklesia*, which means "assembly." Anyone reading the Old Testament in Greek will find *ekklesia* used regularly to refer to God's people assembling in his presence. That same reader who then turns to the pages of the Greek New Testament will continue to see *ekklesia* all over the place, often in connection with God's people assembling in his presence. In other words, since *ekklesia* is used throughout both the Old and New Testaments, anyone reading in Greek can see the answer to the question, "Where do we go today if we want to experience God's unique presence?"

Unfortunately, most English translations (such as the NIV) obscure this connection by using the word "assembly" to translate *qahal/ekklesia* in the Old Testament and then using a completely different English word, such as the word "church," to translate *ekklesia* in the New Testament.[9] But as we have seen, the word translated "church" in the New Testament is the same word translated "assembly" in the Old Testament. Why is this significant? Because today, when we want to experience the jaw-dropping, spine-tingling presence of God as Israel did in the middle of their sacred assemblies, we are supposed to go to church!

JESUS' ASSEMBLY

Understanding this background is helpful when we try to make sense of what Jesus means when he refers to the "church" — the *ekklesia* — in two key places in Matthew's gospel. In Matthew 16:18 Jesus declares, "I will build my church [*ekklesia*]." Jesus is not inventing a new term or a new type of gathering; rather, he is saying: "I will build my *assembly*." He follows this bold statement up with the only other reference he makes to the church while he is on earth (Matt. 18:15–20), concluding with "where two or three are gathered in my name, I am there among them" (NRSV).

The statements Jesus makes about the "church" in the New Testament are exactly what God was saying in the Old Testament. When God's people gathered together around Mount Sinai, around the tabernacle, and around the temple, he was uniquely and powerfully present in their midst. Jesus picks up on this history and informs us that when his followers gather together in his name, just like the visitation of God at Sinai, Jesus will be uniquely and powerfully present in their midst.

The rest of the New Testament builds on these earth-shattering statements of Jesus and unpacks our understanding of what it means to be the assembly of God's people—the church. For example, in 1 Corinthians 5:4 Paul says, "when you are *assembled* in the name of our Lord Jesus ... *and the power of our Lord Jesus is present*" (italics added). Isn't the power of the Lord Jesus present everywhere? Isn't Jesus' power present at the grocery store, the library, or the coffee house? In one sense, the power of Jesus is present everywhere, but, in the church, Jesus' power is uniquely present, because Jesus is with us in a special way when we assemble in his name.

Later in this same letter, Paul lambasts the Corinthian church because when they "came together" as a church to participate in the Lord's Supper, they failed to recognize the unique presence of Jesus with them (1 Cor. 11:23–32). Again, while Jesus is present on the top of Mount Everest, in the middle of the Sahara desert, and in your attic, the Scriptures indicate that he is more *fully* present when his people assemble together for communion.

Likewise, 1 Corinthians 14:23–25 says: "If the whole church *comes together* and ... an unbeliever or someone who does not understand comes in ... he will fall down and worship God, exclaiming, 'God is really among you!'" (italics added). Paul is saying to the church that God's presence is so powerfully experienced in the gathered assembly that even a nonbeliever is able to feel it! Isn't God present at other times in the lives of unbelievers, when they are taking a walk or eating at their favorite restaurant? Why doesn't the unbeliever fall down and worship God at those times? It's because God is *more fully* present in the gathered assembly of God's people.

The uniqueness of God's presence in the assembly is the reason Paul writes to the church of God in Corinth, "Don't you know that you yourselves are God's temple?" (1 Cor. 3:16). In this passage, Paul isn't speaking to us as individuals. While 1 Corinthians 6 does affirm that we are, individually, temples of God's Spirit, the "you" in this passage is plural. Paul is saying to the Corinthian church: "Don't you know that your assembly/church is the temple of God—the means through which God is uniquely present amongst you?" Just as God met with his people in a special way when they assembled around Mount Sinai, the tabernacle, and the temple, today God meets with us wherever and whenever his people gather together in his name as the church.

A woman who had taken her daughter and son-in-law to a church service shared the following testimony with me in an email recently, relating her daughter's impressions of church:

> She was overwhelmed, as was her husband. She had so much to say about the service—the beautiful music and then the wonderful sermon. She said she would not have been able to identify anyone on the platform. All she could identify was the working of the Holy Spirit: "The message was so pure, and given in such a spirit of humility, God spoke so clearly through the pastor, I have never experienced anything to equal it. God is really present in the church." We all felt this way, but hearing it from [our daughter] was confirmation for what [we] have felt all along.

Another woman, visiting another church, described her experience this way: "The first time I came to this church the presence of God was so real in worship that it was almost palpable."[10]

These women experienced God's presence in a unique and powerful way in the gathered assembly.

GOD IN CONCERT

I'd like to suggest that the experience of a concert offers us some insight into the reason why we experience God in a unique way as his gathered people. Consider what happened on February 11, 1963, in Washington D.C., when the Beatles played their first live stage show in America. Eyewitness accounts describe the concert as "breathtaking." The Beatles fed off the energy of the crowd, and the crowd in turn fed off the energy of the Beatles. Paul McCartney later said that it was "the most tremendous reception I have ever heard in all my life." Ringo Starr absolutely reveled in the atmosphere of the evening, playing as never before, and finally exclaiming, "What an audience! I could have played for them all night." For the 18,000 people packed into Washington Coliseum and for the four boys from Liverpool it was pure exhilaration.[11] While the Beatles had performed all of these songs before in their studio and the concertgoers had heard all of these songs before on the radio, something unique happened on that night in 1963.

The same thing happened in the case of Peter Frampton in 1975. Before the early 1970s Peter Frampton had little commercial success as a recording artist. Then in 1975 he played a concert in San Francisco in which the live audience created a unique energy and excitement. The live album produced from that concert was aptly entitled *Peter Frampton Comes Alive* and has sold over sixteen million copies—success not duplicated by anything else Frampton has done. As with the Beatles, it was in concert that Frampton "came alive" and everyone involved experienced his music in a unique and powerful way.

Similarly, in 1987 U2 gathered on the top of a liquor store in Los Angeles to hold an impromptu concert and film a music video. As they played, people from all over the neighborhood and city were drawn into the growing assembly that surrounded the liquor store. The event was immortalized in the music video *Where the Streets Have No Name*. Watching the video, one gets the sense that there was a unique energy and excitement on that day because the band was appearing "live" in concert.

What is it about a concert that makes it such a unique experience for the band and the audience? If a recording can convey the same music, why is it that a concert is often a much more power-ful and exciting experience for the listener? Perhaps you have tried to re-create the concert experience in your living room with an expensive stereo system. You know it just can't be done. It's not that the music is any different. *It's the absence of presence.* The pres-ence of the band and of other fans creates a different experience when the band appears in concert.

Experiencing God in the midst of an assembly, the gathered people of God — his church — is like hearing God in concert. We all, in different ways, experience God throughout our day as indi-viduals: in our private devotional life, in the beauty of nature, and in our acts of service to the poor. But as wonderful and necessary as these experiences are, they do not replace the experience of God in concert. Like an iPod or a portable music player, they replicate the music of the concert experience, but they cannot replace the concert itself. God is a master musician, and he is best experienced live in concert.

THE THEOLOGY OF GOD IN CONCERT

I'd like you to think about heaven for a moment. When the curtain is pulled back and we get a glimpse into the world of heaven in the book of Revelation, we see an enormous assembly — a concert of living creatures, elders, and people of every tribe, nation, and tongue gathered together around the throne of God (Rev. 4–5; 7; 14). Heaven is not presented as a private recital of God's glory. It's not an individualistic experience. When the Bible speaks about the end-time return of Jesus Christ, we are told it is the marriage supper of the Lamb (Rev. 19) — a giant, celebratory, *communal* feast, not a series of private picnics. Heaven is where God is gathered in the midst of his assembled people. It's a com-munity experience.

If you are like most people, you probably tend to think about heaven as something far in the future — a place we go when we die and a reality that has little to do with our life today. But that's not the picture presented in the Bible. While some aspects of our participation with God in heaven are confined to the future, God also tells us that we are *right now* seated with Christ in heavenly places (Eph. 2:6; cf. Col. 3:1 – 2). In other words, in some sense believers are already attending the great concert of heaven.

When we assemble together as the church, we *re-create* the concert of heaven here on earth. Hebrews 12:18 – 29 teaches us that the gathering of God's people is a re-creation of this heavenly experience. Just as Israel gathered around the temple and the tabernacle to re-create their foundational assembly at Mount Sinai, we do something similar when we gather as an assembled church. Instead of re-creating the assembly on Mount Sinai, we join our worship to the eternal worship of the assembled in heaven (Heb. 12:22 – 29). Because we have come near to God in this heavenly assembly, we should "worship God acceptably with reverence and awe" (v. 28).

That is why Hebrews 10:22 – 25 urges us: "Let us draw near to God [and] . . . let us not give up meeting together." The command to worship and the command to assemble go hand in hand. They are not separate commands. When we assemble together here on earth, we draw near to God and are able to worship him acceptably with reverence and awe. In other words, God has given us the church so that we might re-create the assembly of heaven in our gatherings.

There is a second reason why God is more powerfully present in the assembly, and it has to do with the Holy Spirit. The Holy Spirit is God's empowering presence with us. The Spirit indwells each individual Christian, but when we gather together, the Spirit is present among us in a *unique* way (1 Cor. 3:16 – 17; Eph. 2:22).

Consider what it is like to be alone in an unheated room. When you are alone, the only source of heat in the room is your body heat. However, when others join you in the room, they contribute their body heat. Each person brings additional energy and warmth to the room. Likewise, when we are assembled with others, we experience God's presence though his Spirit dwelling in us and in those around us. The addition of others increases our experience of God's presence in a way that is not possible when we meet alone with God.[12]

BUT WHY CHURCH AND NOT SOME OTHER GROUP?

Thus, there is a unique experience of God's presence that comes when we gather together with other believers. But is the blessing present in any gathering, or is there something unique to the gatherings we typically call the church?

In the Old Testament, when it was time to build the tabernacle, God gave incredibly explicit instructions that described exactly what the tabernacle was to be like. These directions were necessary because the earthly structure was a copy — a re-creation — of a heavenly reality. In order for God's people to experience God's presence dwelling among them, the people needed to create *a structure that was built to match God's design.*

Unfortunately, while Moses was away on Mount Sinai receiving detailed instructions from the Lord, the people of Israel became impatient. They wanted God to be accessible to them immediately. They pestered and badgered Aaron into building them a golden calf. Instead of following the painstakingly detailed preparations that God was giving to Moses on the mountain, the Israelites tossed their jewelry into a fire and threw together a golden calf, modeled after Egyptian gods. There was no thought, no planning, and no preparation. Not surprisingly, though the people gathered together as the people of God, when they failed to follow God's design for their gathering, the presence of God was noticeably absent.

Lest we follow in their footsteps, we would do well to remember that it was *Jesus* who said, "I will build my church/assembly" (Matt. 16:18). Jesus didn't tell us to pull any kind of group of Christians together and then wait for him to show up. The promise of his presence is given to the church because it is the institution that Jesus himself has designed to be able to house his presence. Whenever we develop a "golden calf" mentality and grow impatient with God's design or have a desire to control the gathering of God's people, we end up designing and building our own gatherings—not God's. These gatherings are often more of a reflection of the "Egyptian" gods of this world. Unsurprisingly, when we do this we also forfeit the right to experience God in the way he has promised.

As New Testament followers of Christ, we don't follow detailed construction plans to build tents and buildings and objects for worship. Instead, we are called to follow the blueprint of Jesus for the church—his detailed instructions about who is qualified to lead others, how to discipline Christians who have wandered into sin, what is to happen when we gather to celebrate the Lord's Supper, and so on. In other words, God has given us plans for the kind of gathering that will best facilitate his unique presence among us. And it's not just any gathering of Christians. It is the church.

Let's take another look at the idea that the church is God in concert. When you attend a concert, the band or orchestra usually has certain *expectations* when they come to play. They may want to play only certain venues or use a specific kind of sound system. They usually require that someone has done some advertising for the concert or ask that the stage is set up in a certain way. Certainly, they'll want to make sure that someone has sold tickets to the concert. These requirements—expectations for a successful performance—have to be in place to ensure that all who come to the concert enjoy the best experience possible.

When God comes to play a concert, it's no different. His expectations and guidelines for how we can best experience his presence in worship are incorporated into his design for the church, not for other institutions. While God is certainly present in our Christian families, schools, parachurch organizations—and even spontaneous gatherings of Christians on the street—he has promised to be *uniquely* and more *fully* present in the midst of his church, the assembly designed in accordance with his specifications.

SEEING GOD IN CHURCH

We have said so far that God is uniquely present when we gather together as his church. Let me describe for you what that looks like. Sometimes people will come up to me after a sermon and tell me, "God really spoke to me today when you said ..." Then they quote something they heard during the sermon. They may even have the statement written down in their notes! Normally, this would be a great compliment, except for one problem—sometimes I never said what they heard me say! I know this because I write out a manuscript for my sermons, and they are all recorded. I've gone back to check on some of these statements, and I have discovered that quite often, the sentence they attribute to me is in neither the manuscript nor the recording!

The first few times this happened to me, I would gently correct the person and say, "That's great, but what I actually said was this," and I then gave them the statement from the manuscript. Still, even after I had corrected them, people would adamantly argue with me: "Yes, but then you said this!"—and they would point to the sentence in their notes. One day it dawned on me what was happening. We were both right. You see, in addition to the words they were hearing through my prepared sermon, God was also speaking directly to their hearts. These were real, tangible experiences of God speaking to them. That's what happens when God's people gather. God shows up—and he speaks!

The Bible also tells us that God *inhabits* the praise of his people, evoking powerful emotions in their hearts during times of corporate singing. God is present in a unique way when God's people celebrate the Lord's Supper and baptism, whispering to our souls words of correction and hope. One person described such an experience this way: "My Dad and Sue were always asking me to come to church, so finally I did. Little did we know that my first Sunday would be a Communion Sunday. The music played, tears rolled down my face, and I found out why I couldn't fill my brokenness and emptiness. It was because I didn't have Jesus Christ." God's unique presence manifested itself in an overpowering emotional response and the conviction of a need for Jesus.

When Scripture is publicly read aloud, God's voice is heard in the assembly. When God's people pray together, he draws near to them in a powerful way (see Deut. 4:7). When people exercise their spiritual gifts, God manifests his presence (see 1 Cor. 12:7) so that the word of comfort from a person you have just met is truly God speaking to your heart. Singing praises, participating in baptism and the Lord's Supper, hearing God's Word preached, exercising spiritual gifts, and even (at times) praying are meant to be corporate activities, designed to be experienced when God's people *gather together* for worship. And when these things are done together, God's presence is manifested in a unique and powerful way that is tangibly felt.

FAILING TO SEE GOD IN CHURCH

But what about the times when we can't see God in church? I live in Michigan, and after long, cold winters, the summers inevitably involve packing up the kids and heading out to the beach to enjoy some sunshine. Most of the time, this is a great experience for our family. There is just one task that I dread: putting sunscreen on our children. The kids are squirming all over the place while we make a futile attempt at covering them with the lotion. Sometimes they end up covered with more sand than sunscreen. If we miss a spot, it soon becomes blatantly obvious, turning into a painful, red area that leads to constant complaining.

Given my strong dislike for this experience, on cloudy days it is highly tempting for me to skip the sunscreen procedure altogether. But skipping this process is an invitation to disaster — despite the apparent lack of sunshine. Yes, it is still possible to get a sunburn on a cloudy day. The rays of the sun are present, even though we cannot sense their presence the same way we do on a sunny day. Part of maturity—learning to be an adult—is learning to recognize the presence of the sun even when we cannot see it.

There are days when going to church can feel like being outside on a cloudy summer day. You don't feel that immediate warmth of the blazing sun on your skin. The rays of God's love—his visible, manifest presence—feel as if they are hidden behind the clouds. The hair on the back of your neck doesn't stand up during the singing, and there is no specific word from the Lord for your life during the sermon. You may even wonder why you bothered to come to church at all. But just because you can't feel God's presence or sense him at work, it doesn't mean that God is absent. The promise of the Word of God is that whenever his people gather together to worship, receive the Word, and celebrate together, he is present. Some days, his presence is just harder to sense.

The apostle Paul addressed this when he wrote to the church in Corinth in 2 Corinthians 3–4. Some people there were comparing Paul to Moses. They wanted to know why, if Paul was privy to revelations from God, his face didn't glow like Moses' did when he came down from Mount Sinai (Ex. 34). Paul's response is helpful for us to think about as we consider our own longing for the visible, manifest evidence of God's presence. Paul taught the Corinthian church that in the age in which we live, it is not our *outward appearances* that demonstrate the reality of God's presence. Instead, God's work of transformation is primarily an inward experience, as we behold Jesus with the eyes of faith. In other words, we may want outward, visible signs that God is in our midst, but sometimes God's presence is experienced in more subtle ways.

That said, if we never experience God's glory blazing down brightly on our skin, something is amiss. While we should not expect that God will always speak to us with fire igniting our hearts and minds, if he never speaks to us through his Word or draws tangibly nearer to us during corporate prayer, something is wrong. It may be because of unconfessed sin, either in our own lives as individuals or corporately in the church, which will hinder our experience of God's presence, in the same way that an umbrella can hide the sun from us on a sunny day. The sun may be shining, but something is blocking the warmth and light of its rays from reaching us. True and honest confession of our sin is integral to the right functioning of the church, and a biblical church will be certain to practice discipline and admonition of its members.

Still, in the seasons of life, there may be weeks or months where the sun seems to be behind the clouds. Though we should examine our lives and our practice of worship, our failure to experience God does not necessarily mean that he is absent in the assembly. It's during these times that we must go out and put on the "sunscreen" prayer that says, "God, I know you are here. Help me to see you today."

THE PRESENCE OF GOD

Church is certainly not the only means by which God is experienced. God is experienced in nature, through his Word, through prayer, and in our ministry to others. If you decide to live in a mountain village in Asia, read your Bible, serve others, and pray, you will experience God's presence in your life — because God is experienced in each of these ways. Yet something would still be missing from your experience of knowing God — something essential, foundational, and irreplaceable. You would be missing God in concert.

The psalmist pictures for us the unbridled joy of experiencing God in concert in the midst of the gathered assembly:

Come, let's shout praises to GOD,
   raise the roof for the Rock who saved us!
Let's march into his presence singing praises,
   lifting the rafters with our hymns!...

So come, let us worship: bow before him,
    on your knees before God, who made us!
Oh yes, he's our God,
    and we're the people he pastures, the flock he feeds.
Drop everything and listen, listen as he speaks. (Ps. 95:1–2,
    6–7 *MSG*).

Every time his church gathers, God appears in concert. You don't want to miss it.

"SECOND FRIENDS"

Do you have what C. S. Lewis described as "First Friends"? These are the people who resonate completely with you and reveal to you that you are not alone in this world. In a sense, such a person is your alter ego—your twin. Lewis says it this way: "There is nothing to overcome in making him your friend; he and you join like raindrops on a window." Hopefully, we all have friends like this, for they bring immeasurable happiness to our lives. But what about "Second Friends"? Unlike our close alter ego, Lewis describes such a person this way:

> [He is someone] who disagrees with you about everything ... he is not so much the alter ego as the anti-self ... Of course he shares your interests; otherwise he would not become your friend at all. But he has approached them all at a different angle. He has read all the right books but has got the wrong thing out of every one. It is as if he spoke your language but mispronounced it ... When you set out to correct his heresies, you find that he forsooth has decided to correct yours! And then you go at it, hammer and tongs, far into the night, night after night, or walking through a fine country that neither gives glance to, each learning the weight of the other's punches, and often more like mutually respectful enemies than friends. Actually (though it never seems so at the time) you modify one another's thoughts; out of this perpetual dogfight a community of mind and deep affection emerge.[13]

God has designed us to need both kinds of friends, but in some ways our Second Friends are even more important than our First Friends. First Friends help us realize we are not aliens in this world; Second Friends ensure that we do not become mere clones. First Friends reassure us that we are fine just the way we are; Second Friends remind us that we are not. First Friends offer a sense of solidarity; Second Friends provide us with a taste of variety. With First Friends we enjoy warm companionship; with Second Friends we experience true community.

What we are talking about here is the need for diversity in our lives as individuals. We are designed to need relationships with people who are *different* from us. If this is true, where is the best place for us to develop these relationships? In this chapter we want to explore the idea that God has designed the church to give us an opportunity to experience the blessings and benefits that come through these diverse relationships.

DIFFERENT BY DESIGN

The Bible tells us that in the beginning, after creating everything else, God created a man. Although God declared that the man he had made was good, it was *not good* for him to be alone. After searching among all the animals, God did not find a companion suitable for Adam (not even among the dogs!). So God created a woman. The woman was made the same as the man (a human being), but different from the man (female). God certainly could have kept things simple and created another man for Adam. After all, it doesn't seem that the woman was made for purely reproductive reasons. God could have given men that capability, for we know that there are many animals that have asexual reproduction. Instead, God chose to inject the element of *gender diversity* into his creation of human beings.

But God's creative plan for diversity was not limited to gender. Stop and think about this for a moment—what ethnicity were Adam and Eve? Were they Caucasian? Latino? African?

Asian? Let me put the question another way for you. Are Latinos descended from Adam and Eve? Are Africans? Are Asians? Are Caucasians? According to the Bible, all of us, regardless of our ethnicity, are descended from this original couple. God created within Adam and Eve the genetic potentiality for every ethnicity of human beings that now exist on the earth. God designed that from this one couple, the human race would multiply into a wide diversity of ethnicities.

God not only created potential diversity in humanity, he had a plan for unleashing the wide diversity of different ethnicities from one man and woman. In Genesis 9, we read that God commanded Noah and his family to "be fruitful and increase in number and *fill the earth*" (Gen. 9:1, italics added). By scattering human beings to the four corners of the globe, the genetic potential latent in Adam and Eve (and now in Noah and his family) would begin to blossom into various ethnic groups of people.

That began to happen. The descendants of Noah started scattering across the earth. Families developed distinctive patterns of life and unique characteristics. Unsurprisingly, problems began to arise as these diverse ethnic groups scattered. As Noah's descendants were moving toward the east through modern-day Iraq, they decided they didn't want to keep migrating outward. They began to fear the idea of being scattered across the globe. Then, in Genesis 11, they stopped spreading out and settled down at a place called Babel.

Now when I was in Sunday school, I was taught that the problem with the people at Babel was that they wanted to build a tower that stretched all the way to heaven, and God was not happy with their building plans. I'll grant that this is somewhat true, but it obscures the key point of the story. Genesis tells us that the people said to themselves: "Come, let us build ourselves a city, with a tower that reaches to the heavens, so that we may make a name for ourselves and not *be scattered over the face of the whole earth*" (Gen. 11:4, italics added). Yes, the people were proud and wanted to make a name for themselves. But they were also defying God's plans.

God had commanded human beings to migrate outward so that the full range of ethnic diversity latent in his creation could be realized. But the people chose to disobey God's clear command. In response to this disobedience, God decided to frustrate their plans for uniformity and speed up the process of scattering. He created new languages, thwarting the uniformity they had achieved by their own effort, and he dispersed the people by confusing their communication with each other. This scattering of the people at Babel was not simply a punishment for human arrogance; it was God's way of keeping his plan for diversity in creation on track.

If indeed God is committed to diverse ethnic groups spread out across the earth, this raises a more fundamental question: Why did God create diversity in the first place? Wouldn't the world have been a better place if we were all the same? Wouldn't we have less conflict and fewer disagreements? I believe there are four major reasons why God created diversity in the human race.

UNDERSTANDING GOD'S DESIGN IN CREATING DIVERSITY

Loving My Neighbor

The first reason why God intentionally created diversity is that *diversity teaches us to love*. When a lawyer asked Jesus in Luke 10 what was necessary to inherit eternal life, he replied, "Love your neighbor as yourself." Seeking to justify himself, the lawyer responded, "And who is my neighbor?" In response to this, Jesus told the story we commonly know as the parable of the good Samaritan. Though most people think of this as a story about how we need to help those in need, a key point of the story is that the good Samaritan is *different* from the man he helps — and *different* from the people listening to the story. His ethnicity as a Samaritan meant he would not be well-respected by the Jewish listeners (Jews typically despised Samaritans). If Jesus had made the hero in the story a Jew and a close, personal friend of the victim, it would not have served as an adequate representation of God's love. Jesus purposefully made the hero a different (and despised) ethnicity to show us that *the love of God is seen most clearly when it is displayed to someone who is different.*

In case you think I'm reading this into the story, Jesus explicitly highlights this relationship between love and diversity in the Sermon on the Mount: "If you love those who love you, what reward will you get? Are not even the tax collectors doing that? And if you greet only your own people, what are you doing more than others? Do not even pagans do that?" (Matt. 5:46–47 TNIV). The best demonstration of Christian love, according to Jesus, is *loving those who are not like you.* Diversity is a gift from God, an opportunity for us to learn to love as he loves. Commonality gives us an opportunity to *like* others and celebrate what we have in common. Diversity draws us deeper, giving us the chance to truly *love* others in the way God loves others.

Losing Myself with 106,137 of My Closest Friends

In 1991, as a nineteen-year-old college sophomore, I was seated in Section 31 of the Big House at the University of Michigan watching a game between my Michigan Wolverines and the (still) hated Fighting Irish of Notre Dame. A recent series of losses to Notre Dame had been inordinately painful for us, given the glaring mistakes Michigan had made. And this game wasn't looking any better. Our seventeen-point lead had all but evaporated, and it was the fourth quarter. While we were still up 17–14, the momentum had clearly shifted and Notre Dame was on fire. We had the ball at their twenty-five yard line, but the drive had stalled. It was fourth and one, with nine minutes to play. The coach decided to go for it.

The tension in the stadium was palpable. Everyone was expecting a run up the middle. The ball was snapped. Suddenly, horror was mixed with uncontrollable excitement. The quarter-back — Elvis Grbac — was dropping back to pass! Not a single receiver was open, and we all knew that glacially slow Elvis would never run for a first down. He launched a pass, but it looked like he was just throwing the ball away. Suddenly a blur of maize and blue came streaking across the end zone. It was Desmond Howard, Michigan's best receiver. Howard threw himself toward the ball. We gasped. Howard was flying parallel to the ground, arms stretched to their limits. Inches from the turf he locked onto the ball and held on for dear life as he slammed into the ground. Touchdown! The stadium went absolutely crazy. I hugged every-one I could find. Strangers became best friends as we rejoiced together. All around the stadium, 100,000 people were joining in the celebration. I had never felt such a sudden surge of energy, excitement, and enthusiasm. But more than that, this was one of the moments that helped solidify my growing sense of identity as a Michigan Wolverine.

Why did this experience have such a powerful effect on my identity? It wasn't just that I was proud of my team, though I was. It was because the University of Michigan was the one thing that all 106,137 diverse individuals in that stadium had in common. Love of Michigan football brought us together for a brief moment in time. If I had been watching the game at home with my fam-ily, it would have still been an exciting moment, but it is unlikely that it would have had the same effect on my identity. In that moment at the stadium, my identity as a Michigan Wolverine was strengthened and shaped by our shared experience.

This is the second reason why God gave us the gift of diver-sity: it plays a vital role in identity formation. Diverse individu-als gather together when something they have in common draws them together. As they do so, this commonality is highlighted by their differences. It moves to the forefront of their identity. I believe God created diversity, not so that we would find our identity in sports teams or fleeting moments of shared joy, but so that we would find our identity in Jesus as our Creator and Savior. As Jesus draws diverse humanity to himself, he becomes what we have in common and the foundation of our new identities.

The Fellowship of the Ring

The first two books in J. R. R. Tolkien's masterpiece, *The Lord of the Rings*, tell us of a fellowship of diverse individuals united by a common quest.[14] The fellowship was a collection of individuals from diverse backgrounds, all bound together by a common purpose. Four hobbits (small, hairy people with big feet), one wizard, one elf, one dwarf, and two human beings, each with their own strengths and personalities, came together with the goal of destroying a magical ring. As we watch them journey together, we see these diverse individuals being forged into a collective unity. Their unity is strengthened by the diverse sets of talents, experiences, and gifts that each individual brings to the table. But more than that, the diversity of these individuals—the obvious differences they have in ability and background—highlights the unity of their purpose and leads to deep bonds of friendship. Legolas (an elf) and Gimli (a dwarf), at first bitter enemies, become the deepest of friends. This happens, *not in spite of their differences, but because of them.*

This reveals the third reason for our God-given diversity. We experience true community and find greater success in achieving our *common purposes* through diversity. A diverse group is usually more successful because it has a wider set of resources to draw upon. Diversity also facilitates community as we learn to depend on one another, combining our unique gifts, talents, and experiences to achieve this common purpose (we will address this more in chapter 3). God gave us diversity so that we might experience true community and better accomplish his mission in this world. Without a variety of talents, gifts, and perspectives, we would not be able to fully accomplish the mission that God has given us. Our God-designed diversity enables us to fulfill our God-given purpose. (We will address this more in chapter 5.)

A Diverse God

Finally, God created human diversity because God himself is revealed more fully and is glorified more completely through our diversity. Created in his image, our humanity is simply a reflection of the diversity of God. God the Father, God the Son, and God the Spirit are all God, but they eternally exist as three distinct persons. I cannot fully explain the meaning of the Trinity, but I believe it demonstrates at least one key truth about God—there is diversity within the unity of God himself. Because God is a diverse unity of persons, he is more fully revealed and praised through our diversity than he is in bland homogeneity.

The book of Genesis says that God created human beings in his own image, male and female. God, who is neither male nor female, is better represented through men and women than he is through one gender alone. Likewise, since God is neither Caucasian nor Latino, Asian nor African, he is better represented in the diversity of ethnicities than he is through any one, single ethnicity. Furthermore, not only is God better represented by diversity, he is more fully praised when he is praised by males and females than when he is praised just by men; he is more fully praised when he is praised by Africans and Asians than either one alone. The book of Revelation pictures people from *every* tongue and tribe and nation worshiping God at the end of time. The rich tapestry of songs, praises, languages, and expressions manifest on that day will bear witness to God's greatness in a way that no single culture (or gender) could ever do on its own.

These, then, are the four reasons why God created diversity. God created human diversity to teach us to love, to form our identity in Christ, to create community and achieve our mission, and to more fully reveal and glorify our Creator.

UNITY IN DIVERSITY

To achieve these four ends, God could not simply create diversity. The true beauty of diversity is seen only when diverse people come together. It is a beauty recognized in the light of a common unity. If the good Samaritan had never come in contact with the man who needed his help, there would have been no opportunity for love. If I had not gathered at that Michigan stadium with other fans who shared a common desire to see Michigan win the game, there would have been no identity formation. If humans, hobbits, a dwarf, a wizard, and an elf had not come together for the common purpose of destroying the one ring in Tolkien's classic tale, there would have been no community and no accomplishing of their mission. And as long as men and women, Asians and Africans, remain separated from each other, they cannot reveal the true beauty of God and glorify him as fully as possible.

Therefore, it should not surprise us to discover that as soon as God had finished unleashing diversity in Genesis 11, scattering the nations to the four corners of the earth, he also set in motion a plan to eventually bring the diverse peoples of the world back together. In Genesis 12 God begins to unfold his plan to regather the diversity he set in motion in Genesis 11. This plan begins with God's choosing one man, Abraham, and through him one nation, Israel. God intended to use this one person (and the nation that would come from his descendants) to gather all people and all nations to himself (see Gen. 12:2–3; Isa. 66).

If we look at the history of God's people, it is evident that Abraham's descendants failed miserably at their mission of (re-) gathering the nations in worship of God. But in another sense, we see that where the people failed, God succeeded masterfully in accomplishing his greater purposes. Through Abraham and the nation of Israel, Jesus Christ came into this world. And even though the nation of Israel failed, Jesus—the seed of Abraham—was revealed to be God's ultimate plan to gather back a diverse world to himself (Col. 1:20). Just as all the diversity we see in the human race came from one man, Adam, so God planned to unite all this diversity through one man, Jesus.

Paul's letter to the Ephesians tells us that God accomplished this purpose by breaking down the dividing wall of hostility and making peace, unifying people through a common salvation won through the cross of Jesus Christ. Jesus' death and resurrection not only made peace possible between humanity and God, but it also made peace possible between human beings, drawing us out of our hatred and fear to peace and unity in our worship of Jesus (Eph. 2:11–18). Through Jesus, God is redeeming our diversity—not destroying it in the stagnation of uniformity, but creating a beautiful mosaic that highlights and reveals our unity in Christ. Jesus creates unity within the diversity of our genders, ethnicities, and backgrounds because what he accomplished in the work of salvation is for *all* people. All of us, regardless of our differences, find salvation in his *one* body and through *one* Spirit (Eph. 4:4).

So far, so good, right? Well, there's even more. You see, God's plan is not only to make peace among diverse humans a possibility, but an actuality. And God makes this peace a reality as he brings diverse humanity together in the church, the body of Christ.

AN ARMY OF ONE OR ONE ARMY?

God's goal is not just a vague, disembodied, "spiritual" unity. The unity God intends is expressed in physical, visible, bodily ways in this world through the *one body* of Jesus, the church. And that's where we see God's intention for his gathered people. Immediately after the apostle Paul discusses God's plan to unite all people in Christ, he immediately starts talking about the church: "Consequently, you are no longer foreigners and aliens, but fellow citizens with God's people and members of God's household ... In [Christ] the whole building is joined together and rises to become a holy temple in the Lord" (Eph. 2:19–21). Here Paul refers to the universal church, the people of God throughout history, from every generation and nation.

Then, in the next verse, Paul speaks about the importance of the local church: "In him *you too* are being built together to become a dwelling in which God lives by his Spirit" (Eph. 2:22, italics added). In order for us to experience the benefits of this unity, our experience has to be more than a vague, disembodied idea or principle. It has to be located and experienced in time and space. So where do we go to experience the tangible benefits of God uniting our diversity? You find this unity-in-diversity in the local church.[15]

The local church is called "the body of Christ" (1 Cor. 12:27). In other words, God has designed the local church to be the place where we experience this unity-in-diversity we've been talking about. First Corinthians 12:12–13 puts it this way: "The body is a unit, though it is made up of many parts: and though all its parts are many, they form one body. So it is with Christ. For we were all baptized by one Spirit into one body—whether Jews or Greeks, slave or free—and we were all given the one Spirit to drink." Where did God intend people of different ethnic backgrounds (Jew and Greeks) and people of different socioeconomic backgrounds (slave and free) to come together? The local church.

Let's imagine you have ten men and women from diverse backgrounds, ethnicities, age groups, and experiences who want to join the United States Army. They each go to the local recruiter's office and enlist. The moment that they do so, they become members of the US Army. But in order for the army to bring some unity out of the diversity of these recruits, they must now be assigned to a unit because the unit is where they will be forced to interact with each other, develop community, and learn to work together as a team in which each member contributes unique strengths and abilities. This is where they will have their identity reshaped as soldiers in the army. The unit is the community where the army brings unity out of the diversity of its recruits. It's the embodiment of that unity in real, practical, physical ways.

The same is true of the church, but in a deeper and more lasting way. Take, for example, ten men and women from diverse backgrounds, ethnicities, age groups, and experiences who come to acknowledge that Jesus is Lord. The moment they do so, they are enlisted in the universal church, which is made of all believers in Jesus. But, in order to bring unity out of this diversity, God not only has to move in their hearts to acknowledge that Jesus is Lord and enroll them in the universal church, he has to place them together in a local group so that they can learn to love one another and find their identity in Christ alone. They need to learn how to become a community that understands and embraces God's purposes so they can reveal and glorify a diverse God. So God puts these men and women in a unit, a community called the local church.

WHY THE LOCAL CHURCH AND NOT SOME OTHER KIND OF GROUP?

At this point, some might object: why a *local church*? Why not some other group of Christians? I suggest at least three reasons why we need the local church to truly bring unity out of our diversity. First, in order for Christ to redeem our diversity (so that it can accomplish what God originally designed it to reveal), the members of the group in which we are placed cannot have anything else in common except Christ[16] (see the appendix for more on this). God designed the church so that the only criterion for participation is faith in Christ. You don't have to be a college student or be connected with a certain circle of friends. It doesn't matter what your net worth is, what your ethnicity is, or whether or not you have certain abilities and skills. Your education, income level, experience, family background — none of these should prohibit your participation in a local church.

The same is not true of other groups of Christians. For example, in order to participate with an association of Christian lawyers, you have to be a lawyer as well as a Christian. Such a group is not able to fully redeem diversity because such a group cannot embrace every kind of diversity possible.

The church is the only institution that is intentionally designed to accommodate this level of diversity. Families (by their nature) cannot be this diverse; seminaries cannot be this diverse; professional groups cannot be this diverse. Even gatherings of friends cannot be this diverse, as friendship is typically based around common interests and shared experiences. But in the church, friendship is not the *basis* for our unity; rather, it is the *product* of our unity in Christ.

Now, not all churches can be equally diverse. A church at the crossroads of the world in a large, multicultural city has a much greater opportunity to reflect the unity of Christ in the midst of more noticeable diversity than a church in an isolated rural area. However, within any given locality, the church is the organization best suited to embrace the level of diversity present in the community.

The second reason why the church is the place where diversity is best seen and redeemed is that God designed the church so that we could have unity with other Christians regardless of time and geography. The unity God intends for us to experience is not limited by our culture, our location, or the times we live in. The means by which God enables us to experience unity with other believers throughout history and around the world is through the common institution of the church. It doesn't matter if you happened to live in AD 110 or 2010, in Europe or South America, in a large city or a small village. Wherever the gospel has gone, the church has followed. Therefore, when we participate in a local church in America in 2010, we are united with those Christians who participated in a local church in Asia in AD 110.

By contrast, let's say that a group of Christian businessmen decide they no longer want to be part of a local church. They simply want to form their own group with their own rituals and practices (such as flying in Bible teachers, sponsoring conferences, celebrating holidays together, etc.). By rejecting their opportunity to participate in a local church in favor of this new exclusive group they have created, these businessmen cut themselves off from other Christians—not just those in their community, but other Christians around the globe and throughout time. In one sense, they act like army recruits who decide that they would rather develop their own training, design their own uniforms, and set their own rules.

Obviously, the army does not allow such things to happen because it fractures unity. The same is true for the church. In the church we experience unity across space and time because of our common identity in Christ and our common experience of the Spirit. At a minimum, this includes our participation in the Spirit-formed community of God's church. Even in AD 110, a Christian living in Asia could gather with other Christians, celebrate communion and baptism, hear the Word preached, pray with other believers, share financial resources with those in need, and sing praise to God. As followers of Christ today and members of his church, we share in these same experiences and share a level of unity with believers from all times and places.

There is a third reason why the church is better suited for bringing unity out of diversity. One of the blessings of diversity is that it allows for differing ways of viewing God and his truth. Where would we be, for example, if we had only the gospel of Mark to tell us about Jesus, and not Matthew, Luke, and John? How much less would we understand about the doctrine of justification by faith if we had only the letters of Paul or only the words of James? This is one of the great blessings of diversity.

However, with this blessing comes an associated danger. Some of the different ways of viewing God and his truth are incorrect. While the four Gospels in our New Testament give a fuller view of Jesus' life and ministry, there were many other gospels not included in our New Testament whose picture of Jesus is false. While Paul and James give complimentary views of justification by faith, others have introduced misleading views of justification by faith. How are Christians to sort through what is true and what is false?

Ironically, the first theological issue that the early Christians faced was an issue related to ethnic diversity (Acts 15)! Some in the early church were arguing that only those who agreed to be circumcised (a key distinguishing feature of the Jewish people) could be saved. Others were arguing that Gentiles could be believers in Christ without adopting Jewish circumcision. How did they resolve this issue? They took the matter to the Jerusalem church. The discussion included representatives of the differing positions as well as the leadership of the church. During the discussion the blessings of diversity became evident as different people with different experiences, backgrounds, and understandings of Scripture came together, and God revealed his will in and through their diversity. The pattern established by Acts 15 is that the church is best suited to evaluate diverse theological viewpoints that naturally arise because of diversity.

While churches do not always handle theological differences correctly (as evidenced by the embarrassing number of divisions and denominations within Christianity), they often have. Acts 15 is just the first of many examples of how the church through God's grace has brought theological unity out of different theological positions. Because local churches are united with other churches through time and space and because local churches are themselves filled with those with different gifts, experiences, and backgrounds, the local church is best equipped to both present a more complete picture of God and his truth as well as to navigate through the dangers of theological error.

BUT MY CHURCH IS NOT VERY DIVERSE

Often, the ease with which we form First Friends (those similar to us) often precludes us from putting in the time and effort necessary to develop Second Friends (those different from us). This is no different in the church. Though we've highlighted God's purposes for the church, the sad reality is that it is still much easier to seek uniformity rather than unity-in-diversity. It is more practical to organize our churches around commonalities rather than trying to overcome our differences. It is more attractive (and often more cost-effective) to market ourselves to a niche than to target all people. The church, of all places, must resist the temptation to compromise its calling and identity—or it will be robbed of the power it has to redeem our diversity. Unfortunately this is often not the case. We cannot resist the siren song of similarity. So we need to admit honestly that our churches are not as diverse as they could be.

Yet despite our failures, God has designed into the church a level of diversity that we have only diminished, not completely destroyed. There is often more diversity in our churches than we might notice at first glance. This is because we are conditioned to think primarily about ethnicity when we consider diversity. The church reflects diversity, not just in ethnicity, but in different genders, ages, experiences, giftedness, backgrounds, occupations, and socioeconomic status. Most churches may still struggle with appropriate levels of diversity in these areas, but an honest assessment of the church reveals that in all our weakness and failure, we have not been able to overcome the inherent design God intends for his gathered people.

A church that truly unifies around the acknowledgment that Jesus is Lord, even in the most homogenous of communities, will still exhibit some diversity in its membership. And the diversity in some of the most homogenous churches is still far greater than most other Christian organizations. Even with all its problems and weaknesses, the church is still the best institution to achieve the goal of redeeming our diversity for the glory of God.

DESPISING DIVERSITY, DESPISING CHURCH

In 1 Corinthians 11, Paul addresses a specific problem that arose when the church in Corinth gathered together for communion. In the church were rich people and poor people. Yet, when it was time for them to come together and celebrate the Lord's Supper — the sign of their common salvation through Christ — the rich people brought food with them to eat before celebrating communion. They enjoyed a social outing, a luxury of their wealth. They ate, drank, and celebrated together. Those who were poor did not have food to eat and were unable to share in the preparty celebration. A meal intended to highlight their unity became, instead, a sign of their sinful, selfish behavior.

Paul, furious at this behavior, didn't hold back in his criticism. He did not begrudge the wealthy their right to enjoy their own food, but he commanded that they eat their meals at home. When the whole church gathered together to celebrate the Lord's Supper, this was the time when unity — not division — should be clearly reflected. As Paul writes in 1 Corinthians 10:17, "Because there is one loaf, we, who are many, are one body, for we all partake of the one loaf." The very act of sharing communion was designed to bring unity out of our diversity.

Note, however, that as Paul scolds the rich Corinthians, he does not say, "You are despising the rite of the Lord's Supper." He says, "You despise *the church of God*" (1 Cor. 11:22, italics added). In other words, the Corinthians' divisive actions before and during the Lord's Supper were robbing the church of its power to bring unity out of diversity. The Corinthians had failed to recognize the inherent power and design of the church, namely, that it was God's community for uniting the rich and the poor of Corinth (as well as the Jews and Gentiles, the slaves and the free, 1 Cor. 12:13). Paul's warning to them is also a warning to us today: we must not despise the ability of church to redeem our diversity.

FINDING MYSELF WITH A HUNDRED OF MY CLOSEST FRIENDS

In addition to attending football games, there were other things I did in college. Every Sunday morning I would invariably get up later than I intended, jump in the shower, get dressed as fast as possible, and rush down the stairs. Typically, everyone else in the apartment building was asleep. Outside, there was an old Buick waiting for me, driven by a man named James. Often, his wife, Betty, and their young children, Anna and James Jr., would be there too. James and I didn't have much in common. He was a parole officer and I was an engineering student. He was in his thirties and I was a teenager. He had a family and I was single. He was black and I was Arab. He was soft-spoken and I was boisterous.

But every Sunday he was there, waiting to pick me up for church. We went to our little, one-hundred-member church and worshiped the Lord together. Then he drove me home. There wasn't always a lot of conversation in the car while we drove. But my life was richer because I knew James and his family. I understood that the God I loved and served was not just my personal God, but the God of this black, thirty-something, married parole officer. James and I didn't always see God the same way, and I learned that there were different ways to understand who God was — and still remain faithful to the truth of Scripture. When we talked, we often talked about our common goal of seeing the kingdom of God come. Though in many ways we were different, I felt closer to James than I did to many of my roommates or the thousands of other people at the University of Michigan.

That's the beauty of the church. It is the means by which God brought James and me together. By uniting our diversity, God was providing the opportunity for us to learn to love as he loves, to find our identity in Christ alone, and to develop true community and accomplish the mission of God together. I am convinced that God was more glorified because James and I were worshiping him together rather than apart.

CHAPTER 3

THE CITY

City of the damned lost children with dirty faces
No one really seems to care[17]

"You will be a restless wanderer on the earth" (Gen. 4:12). When Cain killed his brother Abel in Genesis 4, this was God's punishment — a life of loneliness, the inability of finding the home he longed for among the community of God's people. Because Cain had despised and destroyed his relationship with his brother, he reaped the consequences of his sin, becoming a restless wanderer and fearing for his life, unable to trust others.

Immediately, Cain sensed the true depth of his loss: "My punishment is more than I can bear," he complained to God. "Today you are driving me from the land, and I will be hidden from your presence; I will be a restless wanderer on the earth, and whoever finds me will kill me" (Gen. 4:13–14). God, with great mercy, recognized Cain's need for safety and marked Cain so that no one would kill him. But God did nothing to alleviate the punishment of being a restless wanderer. So Cain took matters into his own hands and tried to fill the emptiness in his life by creating something to meet his need, that would lift the curse on his life. Cain built the first city in human history. He gathered people around him, making a community for himself, a home to replace the one he lost, relationships to replace the brother he killed. Instead of being a restless wanderer, Cain looked to the city he created to provide a home where he could belong.

The experience of loneliness is not limited to Cain. Our sinful and selfish choices in life make us all restless wanderers to some extent. Our refusal to submit to God's direction for our lives creates rifts, not only with God but also with those around us.

And like Cain, we cannot bear our empty existence as restless wanderers, so we attempt to create our own communities to help us overcome our alienation and our loneliness. We try to find community in our schools, with our sports teams, on social networking sites, in chat rooms, at local hangouts, in virtual worlds, and in urban communities. Wherever we look to belong, wherever we seek to address the curse of Cain in our lives, we are creating a "city" of our own making—a city designed to meet our needs and to end our loneliness and alienation. Like Cain, we build and belong to these cities, trying desperately to overcome our status as restless wanderers.

Literal cities represent the pinnacle of our attempts to establish communities where we can belong and find freedom from the curse. They are designed to allow us to work, eat, socialize, and live in neighborhoods with others; they are our best attempt at regaining what was lost, the union of our lives with others in significant and meaningful work. But have we succeeded? Have our own hands produced the community we desperately long for?

THE CITY OF MAN

Not surprisingly, the city Cain created and the cities we create, far from meeting our needs, only highlight our failure to create real, lasting community. Instead of being the place of authentic community, the city is the place of anonymity—the very pinnacle of the curse itself. In loneliness, we spend our days rubbing shoulders on the street with people we do not know, getting lost in governmental bureaucracies, laboring for corporate leaders who do not know our names, buying and selling from strangers in the marketplace, and being contacted by people (and computers) who pretend to know us.[18] Green Day, in their song "Jesus of Suburbia," laments the city of the damned where all are lost and no one cares. Jim Morrison of the Doors bemoans the mysterious L.A. Woman, another lost angel, alone in the city of night.[19] Jacques Ellul calls the city the "place of non-communication,"[20] and Martin Heidegger refers to the city as the gravitational center of planetary homelessness.[21]

Our virtual cities are no better at meeting our desperate need for community. Quentin Schultze notes that cyberspace communities are "little more than interest groups, demographic colonies, or what Daniel J. Boorstin calls 'consumption communities.'"[22] Instead of being the solution to the relational problems created by the fall, the city has exacerbated our longings and has itself become a symbol of humanity's collective loneliness. We have created the city, but we have failed to achieve community. Despite the proliferation of social networking sites, coffee houses, and the growth of cities like New York and Beijing, we are still just restless wanderers, alone in a crowd of billions.

THE CITY OF GOD

God does not want us to remain restless wanderers like Cain. While our feeble attempts to create community for ourselves in human cities have failed, God has not ignored or condemned these efforts. Instead, he is actively promoting his alternative, a city of his own creation: the City of God—a place where men and women can once again live in peace with each other and with God. In the Old Testament, the City of God was uniquely associated with the historical city of Jerusalem (Ps. 48), the place where the wandering Israelites finally settled, where a permanent home for God was built, and where God was uniquely present.

But the ancient city of Jerusalem was always meant to point to a far greater reality—a reality not exclusively tied to any earthly city. In Galatians 4:21–31, Paul writes that the historical city of Jerusalem represents a heavenly city, where God is right now dwelling in the midst of his people. This heavenly city is a place where restless wanderers find rest and where the lonely find true community. Dwelling in the City of God is our future hope (Rev. 21:2), something all Christians are longing for (Heb. 13:14) — whether we know it or not.

According to the author of Hebrews, Abraham longed for this city God had prepared for him — the heavenly City of God — because he sensed he was an alien and stranger on this earth (Heb. 11:13). Is that *our* fate as well? Are the followers of Jesus called to be restless wanderers, waiting for the arrival of this heavenly city before we can know the joy of being home?

Thank God, the answer is no! Although in one sense we still remain "aliens and strangers in the world" until Christ returns (1 Pet. 2:11), God has created a community for us, a community where we "are no longer foreigners and aliens" (Eph. 2:19). He has created a new community of people by reconciling us to himself and to one another in and through the body of Christ (Eph. 2:16 – 18). Today, as we await the complete arrival of the heavenly city, God gives us the gift of the local church, which is the manifestation of the City of God in this age and therefore the means for us to experience true community today.

THE ONLY COMMUNITY CALLED "COMMUNITY"

Most of us probably don't have to travel far to find a coffeehouse. Over the past decade, coffeehouses have opened up everywhere, with names ranging from the ubiquitous Starbucks to the more unique, local coffeehouses, such as Madcap (my wife's favorite coffeehouse in Grand Rapids). To my knowledge, most American coffeehouses rarely have Greek names — with one major exception: *koinonia*. A quick Google search reveals coffeehouses with this name all over the country, from San Francisco to Mississippi. Why do so many coffeehouses choose this Greek word when naming their business? *Koinonia* is an ancient Greek word that incorporates the ideas of "community," "relationship," "fellowship," "sharing," and "partnership." As smart coffeehouse owners know, people don't just come to their establishment to drink coffee; they come to develop relationships with other people.

In ancient Greek, *koinonia* was a word that described the closest personal relationships; it named the inextricable intertwining of individual lives. *Koinonia* described things held jointly in common; the term was used to refer to marriage relationships, business partnerships, and close friendships—especially between those who shared a common mission. Perhaps most important for our discussion, when Greek speakers wanted to talk about the interwoven matrix of lives that created the common, shared life of people in a city, they used the word *koinonia*.

Since *koinonia* was such a key word in the ancient Greek language to refer to relationship, partnership, fellowship, sharing, and community, it is not surprising that this word is frequently found throughout the New Testament (which was written in Greek). Yet when we study the word *koinonia* in the New Testament, though it had a wide range of uses in the Greek culture, there is only one community that is named using this powerful term. Both Acts 2:42 and 1 Corinthians 1:9 use the term as a title for the *local church*.[23]

In other words, while coffeehouses are places where you can *find* community, church *is* community. The joining of individual lives, unified by a common experience of salvation, by the life of the Holy Spirit, and by a shared sense of mission, is so essential to his design of the local church that God simply refers to the church by this common Greek word, *koinonia*— *"the community."* It's almost as if God is telling us that all other relationships, partnerships, and communal affiliations are shadows of the real thing, the church— the place where God provides the means to change us from restless wanderers and to give us true community with his people.

GOD'S CREATION

While the Scriptures clearly highlight the local church as the place where God intends us to find community, why should this be the case? To answer this question, we must consider the mess that led to our restless wandering in the first place. Cain failed (as we all do) to love God and his brother—choosing instead to love himself. Self-centered love always prohibits and even destroys true community. But Cain's choice was not just a one-time act by an isolated individual. It is the fruit of our fallen condition, an experience common to the entire human race. We are, without exception, filled with selfishness. No one has to teach a small child to be selfish—it comes naturally to every one of us.

God knows that because we are plagued with this disease of self-love, any city we create will also be infected with selfishness and will lead to brokenness, strife, and even murder. The problem with Cain's city was not that it was a city; it was that Cain was the one who designed and built it. The problem with our sports teams, schools, businesses, and civic organizations is not that it is wrong to gather with others to seek community. The problem is that all of these attempts at community have been designed and built by selfish, fallen human beings. What chance do we really have of solving the problem of our own selfishness? What hope do we have of overcoming the inborn tendency to put our own needs and desires before those of others? Christians are simply people who readily admit that we cannot design a solution to the problem of our sin. Instead, we must rely entirely on God to bring us a salvation that is not of our own doing. Only God can provide restless wanderers with a home. Only God can turn selfish people into lovers of God and others.

In the church, God has designed an organization that at the same time uniquely addresses our distance from God and others, which results from our ongoing sin and selfishness. As we saw in chapter 1, the church is the means by which God is uniquely present. And chapter 2 showed us that the church is the way God is drawing together diverse humans and teaching us to truly love our neighbors. Therefore, because the church is about loving God and loving others, it alone among communities in this world truly addresses the problem of loneliness by countering the self-ish tendencies that made us restless wanderers in the first place. Sports teams, book clubs, schools, and civic groups all have their purpose, but none of them is fundamentally about loving God and loving others. Each one in its own way is infected with our inescapable bent toward selfishness because, like Cain's city, they are the product of human efforts to achieve community. But the church is God's solution to the problem of our loneliness.

REJOICING TOGETHER, WEEPING TOGETHER

In Dallas a few years ago, a little five-year-old boy went into his mother's room. He tried and tried to wake her, but she just wouldn't get up. Failing to wake her, the little boy went to get his grandparents — the woman's parents — to ask for help. They entered the room and were shocked to discover that their daughter — twenty-nine years old and in great health — had somehow died in her sleep. To this day, no one really knows why she died. The little boy didn't understand what was happening, but the young woman's family was immediately rocked with grief — especially her older sister. The two sisters had been close, talking together every day on the phone and frequently spending time together. Now the younger sister was gone, leaving behind a lost little boy.

Unfortunately, stories like these are all too common. Sometimes we read them on the Internet and feel a sense of sadness and empathy for those who are suffering, but typically that sadness passes and we return to our lives. I found out about this particular story after a phone call from my brother. I could tell by his voice that this was not a routine phone call. The woman who died was his sister-in-law, and his wife was the desperately grieving older sister. Their lives were devastated by this tragedy, and to this day my brother and his wife bear the wounds of their suffering.

For my brother, the passing of a twenty-nine-year-old woman would have just been another tragic, unfortunate story, but for one key difference—years earlier he had married into the family. He would probably have never met the woman who died or known much about her, but when he married her sister, a new relationship was created. Though the relationship with his sister-in-law developed over several years, in one sense it was there from the moment he married his wife.

This is what happens when we become children of God. Suddenly, because we have been adopted by God, we find that we are now in a new relationship with all of God's other children. It doesn't matter if we feel anything in these relationships or not— these are real relationships created by God. To facilitate these relationships, God created the church. The church is "family time," an opportunity for God's family to come together and become *in practice* what we have been declared by God to be.

In 1 Corinthians 12:26 Paul says of the local church, "If one part suffers, every part suffers with it; if one part is honored, every part rejoices with it." Paul is not saying that we *should* suffer and rejoice with others in the church; rather, he is saying that we *will*. Everyone who is truly part of this community will have their lives inextricably linked to others. Like a close-knit family, when one of us suffers a loss, we will all experience it.

As I was growing up, my family ate dinner together as often as possible. But we didn't eat dinner to *establish* new relationships with each other. After all, the dinner wasn't what made us a family; it was the fact that we'd been born to the same parents. We shared dinner together to experience and develop the relationships that already existed (and, of course, to eat food). God created the family as the community that best facilitates these types of sibling relationships. In families, siblings who have different interests, gifts, and skills come together on the basis of an established relationship that already exists. In much the same way, God does not urge us to participate in the church so that we can *establish* relationships with other Christians. We participate in the church to develop and enjoy the relationships that already exist, that have been created by God. The church is the means by which God wants to facilitate our relationships with other believers. Without the local church, we are orphaned, separated from the key family relationships that God has given us to help us overcome our loneliness.

How does this happen? We will look at four of the most important ways the church helps us develop community with others.

DEVELOPING COMMUNITY WITH OTHERS IN THE CHURCH

Eating Together

One primary way we can get to know our neighbors is by sharing a meal with them. Whether it is a neighborhood block party, a dinner for eight, or a simple picnic, bonds of community are inevitably formed during shared meals. The same is true when we gather as the community of God's people. Throughout history, Christians have shared meals with one another. It may be a potluck, a small group dinner, or another gathering with other believers, but when we share a meal together, we experience deeper bonds of community.

Now there is nothing unique or special about church members sharing a meal, but God has also designed a special meal, uniquely for those in the church, which allows us to forge deeper relationships with God and with each other. It's called the Lord's Supper, Communion, or the Eucharist. It's a meal that forms community, making us participants with other believers and with God, and it is a spiritual celebration of God's saving work in Christ. Referring to this meal, the apostle Paul writes: "Is not the cup of thanksgiving ... a participation (*koinonia*) in the blood of Christ? And is not the bread that we break a participation (*koinonia*) in the body of Christ? Because there is one loaf, we, who are many, are one body, for we all partake of the one loaf" (1 Cor. 10:16–17). The Lord's Supper is a gift that God gives to the local church to help us develop unity in our relationships as his people.

The church is truly "the community" (*koinonia*, the word we looked at earlier) when it is celebrating the supper of the Lord. In Acts 2:42–45, the church is called the community while they are celebrating the Lord's Supper together. In 1 Corinthians, where Paul criticizes the church for not living out the reality of the community, it is due to the fact that they are abusing the Lord's Supper (1 Cor. 11:17–22) and not celebrating it in the way God intended. When the community eats the Lord's Supper together in the way God intended, true community develops as the Lord is present in a unique way with his people, drawing all who participate closer to himself and to each other.

Embracing Strangers at the City Gate

In 2001, my wife, Lisa, and I went to England to visit a number of different schools to explore God's leading regarding additional studies. One of the pastors in our church had a connection with a wonderful Baptist church located in the middle of London. With his assistance we were able to stay at the church for a portion of our trip. We arrived at the church on a Saturday night, and though we were tired, the next morning we attended the church service. I'll admit that it was partly out of a sense of obligation for our lodging!

During the service we were introduced to the congregation, and afterward a couple came rushing up to meet us. Greg and Marian were Americans who had been living in England for the past two years, and they immediately invited us to come and stay at their home, where there would be more room for us and an opportunity to enjoy some home-cooked meals. Greg even offered us a mobile phone to use during our stay in England. We tried to refuse — after all, we had never seen these people before — but they insisted, and we gratefully accepted their offer. They welcomed us into their home and showered us with hospitality. After our trip, we kept in touch. The following year we moved to Oxford and over the course of our time in England, we stayed with them countless times, often joining them for worship at the Baptist church. They became the dearest of friends and are now godparents to all our children, all because of a simple offer of loving hospitality.

Such is the power of hospitality to form deep relationships among fellow Christians. In Romans 12, God commands that we "share (*koinoneo*, the verb associated with *koinonia*) with God's people who are in need. Practice hospitality" (12:13). The practice of hospitality is not about entertaining those we know (as we commonly assume); it's about embracing strangers! And although hospitality most often happens in the home, the practice of hospitality truly "flourishes at the intersection of the personal, intimate characteristics of the home and the transforming expectations of the church."[24] The church serves as the "city gate," the front door where initial contacts between people are made. Travelling Christians, individuals new to town, or those who simply feel "lost" can go to the church, a place where any stranger is welcome.

Through loving, Christian hospitality, restless wanderers come to experience true community. Unlike hospitals, nursing homes, and hotels, there is no difference in status between those giving and those receiving hospitality — all are one in Christ. In the church, we are all strangers and aliens, and we are all servants of one another. *Koinonia* — the community of God's people — is enhanced as we open up our lives and homes without regard to status or standing.

Sharing with Those in Need

In addition to the Lord's Supper and the practice of hospitality, we come to experience community with other believers through the sharing of our resources with those in need. Hebrews 13:14 – 16 says, "For here we do not have an enduring city, but we are looking for the city that is to come. Through Jesus, therefore, let us continually offer to God a sacrifice of praise — the fruit of lips that confess his name. And do not forget to do good and to share (*koinonia*) with others, for with such sacrifices God is pleased."

In the last chapter we argued that diversity is part of God's plan for creation. In a diverse gathering of people individual members have more to offer one another precisely because they are so different from each other. For example, in an economically diverse group there will be opportunities for those who are well-off to share with those who are in need. In 1 Timothy 6:18 Paul commands those who are rich in this world to be "willing to share" (a word related to *koinonia*). If your only experience of Christian community is a gathering of well-off friends, sharing financial resources is unnecessary. But in the church, amidst economic diversity, there will be the opportunity to develop the deep relationships that come through financial generosity.

In a similar way, church provides unique opportunities to share the wisdom of our experiences, offering comfort and assurance to those who struggle. Second Corinthians 1:7 says that we are to "share" (*koinoneo*) with one another the comfort that we ourselves have received from God. If your only experience of Christian community is in a fellowship of Christian college students, this group will be well equipped to comfort you through the struggle of choosing your classes or dealing with persecution from a professor. But where would you turn if you were diagnosed with cancer? What is the likelihood that someone else in your college group has faced that? The church that God has created is multigenerational, allowing us to draw from the experience of Christians in every stage of life.

Churches that reflect this aspect of the body of Christ are more likely to have others who have already walked the difficult road of cancer. And the comfort this brother or sister in Christ can offer you will encourage you in your suffering and allow you both to experience the deep bonds of friendship as your emotional, spiritual, and practical needs are met by another brother or sister in the family of God. Who among us doesn't need this?

Walking in the Light

Have you ever attended a school where you didn't know any other Christians? Or have you worked in an office where you thought you were the only believer? While many of us have friends who are not Christians, there is often a sense that something is missing in our relationships. As we struggle to live out our Christian faith, our non-Christian friends and coworkers are living for themselves. The difference between these two aims causes a feeling of distance and separation. This is not surprising because God tells us that it is impossible for light and darkness to truly experience community together; as close as our friendships may seem at times, no true *koinonia* is possible between those who are believers in Jesus and those who are not (2 Cor 6:15).

Conversely, have you ever been part of a group of Christians who were serious about their faith, endeavoring to live in light of God's commands and working diligently to hold each other accountable? A deep sense of friendship and community forms. God promises that if we "walk in the light," we will experience true community (*koinonia*) with him and with each other (1 John 1:3–7). The final way in which the church establishes authentic community is by enabling us to strive together to be more like Christ: walking together in the light of God's truth.

This may be best illustrated by the twelve disciples of Jesus, who prefigure the church. While some of the twelve were from the same family (Peter and Andrew, James and John) and some were from the same hometown (Peter, Andrew, and Philip), most were not familiar with each other at the beginning of Jesus' ministry. However, by the end, this group of disciples had developed deep relationships with each other. As they drew closer to Jesus, they drew closer to each other. In his first letter, John is saying that as we labor with others to be more like Jesus, we develop close relationships with our fellow travelers. In the next chapter we will learn that the church is uniquely designed to make us more like Christ and therefore is the place where we develop community as we walk together in the light.

MORE FAMILY THAN FAMILY

Earlier I used the example of the family to help us understand our relationship to one another in the church. But if God created the family, why do we need the church? Isn't the family the primary place where God wants us to find true community and develop deep and lasting relationships with others? While the cities of man are our own creations, the family is clearly a creation of God. If we have loving Christian families, why do we need the church?

In ancient Judaism the family was, indeed, the primary place of community. It was the basic building block of culture and society; family relationships were treasured and honored above all other relationships. Imagine the shock, then, of the person who approached Jesus in Matthew 12 as he was teaching a crowd in Galilee. Normally, it would be rude to interrupt a teacher while he was speaking, but this messenger is convinced he has news of utmost importance. Bursting into the room while Jesus is speaking, the messenger blurts out, "Your mother and brothers are standing outside, wanting to speak to you." Rather than stopping his talk and going to meet them, Jesus turns to the man and asks him a shocking, almost offensive question: "Who is my mother, and who are my brothers?" Then Jesus points to his disciples and followers and calmly states: "Here are my mother and my brothers. For whoever does the will of my Father in heaven is my brother and sister and mother."

In that moment, Jesus, by his actions and his words, subverted the most important institution in Judaism — the family — and replaced it with something new. What could possibly outrank the family? What could be more important and significant than the relationships formed by blood, birth, and marriage? Jesus' answer is clear: the relationships between people who are committed to doing the will of the Father in heaven, the community of his disciples — the church.

This was more than a brief teaching point for Jesus; it reflected his core message. Those closest to Jesus while he was on earth were not the members of his own family. Jesus established *koinonia* with those who had given up everything for the sake of the kingdom of God. This idea of a new and better community is the basis of the promise we find in Mark 10:29–30. When Jesus speaks with a young wealthy man of authority, he asks him to leave his wealth to follow Jesus, just as his disciples have done. Recognizing the hardship of leaving family and wealth behind, Jesus then declares, "No one who has left home or brothers or sisters or mother or father or children or fields for me and for the gospel will fail to receive a hundred times as much in this present age (homes, brothers, sisters, mothers, children and fields — and with them, persecutions) and in the age to come, eternal life."

What does it mean to receive "homes, brothers, sisters, mothers, children and fields" in this present age? This is not a promise that God will bless those who follow him with happy marriages, lots of children, large families, and much property. Instead, Jesus is speaking of a new family, a family of faith called the church, where one has access to hundreds of different homes and fields (through Christian hospitality) and hundreds of brothers, sisters, mothers, and children who share a common relationship to God the Father through his Son, Jesus Christ. The promise of Jesus, the reward to those who leave everything to follow him, is fulfilled in this new community — the church. While earthly families of flesh and blood still serve an important purpose in God's plan, the family of God — his church — now has pride of place among all the social groups of the world, surpassing even the family.

WHY DON'T I FEEL MORE COMMUNITY IN CHURCH?

As great as the church sounds, we need to be honest and admit that it doesn't always live up to our expectations. The community created by God doesn't always feel like home. It isn't always a place of deep and lasting relationships, where we grow with other believers.

Why is that? Just as we saw four ways that the church deepens our experience of community, there are also four things that can hinder this experience. The first hindrance is the depth of our own *koinonia*, our own communion, with God. For many of us, God plays a secondary role in our lives. We naturally tend to feel more affinity with those on our soccer teams, with other parents, and with people at work because our leisure, our children, and our work easily become more central to our lives than God.

The natural affinity we feel in these groups, however, often falls short of the depth that God wants us to experience in the church. We often allow ourselves to settle for a shallow form of community with others, a community of like interests and shared affinities, while we miss the deep *koinonia* that comes from passionately pursuing God with other believers. Sadly, too often our desires for God are weak and halfhearted, with the result that our participation in the community of faith often lacks the depth that God wants it to have. Our church community is shallow because our relationship with God is shallow.

A second hindrance to community, particularly in America, is the isolation we create for ourselves and the value we place on living independent from others. The myth of the rugged, individualistic American is antithetical to the experience of true community.

In graduate school, one of my professors shared his life story in a chapel service. He had recently moved back to America after living a number of years in Poland, where he had labored with Polish believers to establish a seminary. As he talked about the people and events that had mattered to him, he became visibly agitated and sorrowful as he recalled moving from Poland back to America. He began to lament the vapidity and superficiality of American relationships, relative to what he had experienced in Poland. I could feel his pain and anger. And he was right. Even in the church, we often choose to exalt the values of individualism and self-reliance. Why bother to share our deepest needs with others when we can fix our problems ourselves? As a result, we remain restless wanderers missing out on true *koinonia*.

Third, we fail to experience true community because our level of commitment is weak. We jump from church to church and from relationship to relationship, looking for people who will feed our own sinful, selfish tendencies. The paradigmatic city created by human beings that we find in the Bible is the city of Babylon. Babylon has a long and interesting history, a city that began in Genesis 11 in human rebellion against God and rises to become Babylon the Great at the end of time (Rev. 17–18). Interestingly, the chief characteristic of Babylon the Great is that she is the "mother of prostitutes" and the place of adultery.

Why do the human cities fail to provide us with true community? Largely because they, like prostitutes and adulterers, choose the path of ease and instant gratification over the blessings of long-term commitment. Just as God designed sex to give us ultimate joy and intimacy in the context of a marriage relationship, the true intimacy of relationships in the church is best experienced in the context of a long-term commitment. We long to enjoy community, but we want it to be easy, without strings attached. We want intimacy and depth without sacrifice and commitment. Like serial daters, we refuse to join a church or get involved because we are always waiting to see if something better will come along. As church members, we abandon our church with little hesitation when problems or difficulties arise, or if we discover something more exciting, relevant, or pleasing to us.

While many Christians rightly denounce pornography, adultery, and prostitution, how many of us think twice about church hopping? Although pornography, adultery, and prostitution are radically more abhorrent to God than church-hopping, in many ways the same spirit animates both classes of actions — gratification of our selfish desires in contrast to the long-term commitment of a covenant relationship.

Fourth, we fail to experience community by the way we engage in church activities and programs at the expense of relationships. Far too often, church leaders and members prioritize tasks and activities over spending meaningful time with others. We emphasize programming over people, and rituals over relationships. Amy Dickinson, in her book *The Mighty Queens of Freeville*, describes two different church experiences. Dickinson grew up attending the small-town Freeville United Methodist Church, but now lives with her daughter in Washington, D.C., and attends Christ Episcopal Church. In her book she narrates a return visit to the United Methodist Church of Freeville and describes the "joys and concerns" prayer time during the service, the living nativity, and the potluck suppers. In comparing the two churches, Amy opines, "We left our big city church, with its staff of well-trained clergy, its historical significance, large endowment, and massive charity efforts, and came home to a place that doesn't do communion very well but excels at community."[25]

Admittedly, Amy's positive view of community is likely more a result of sentimentality than substance, but she still manages to put her finger on an important truth. Some churches' organizational strengths and liturgical prowess hinder the experience of community.

EARLY CHRISTIANS IN THE CITY

E. R. Dodds, a prominent historian, examined early Christian churches in order to look for reasons why Christianity spread so quickly in its early years. After comparing Christianity with several other religious groups, Dodds concludes: "A Christian congregation was from the first a community in a much fuller sense than any corresponding group of Isiac or Mithraist [pagan religious groups] devotees. Its members were bound together not only by common rites but by a common way of life." This sense of belonging was even more important than the material help that Christians provided one another through church. Dodds concludes:

> Modern social studies have brought home to us the universality of the "need to belong" and the unexpected ways in which it can influence human behavior, particularly among the rootless inhabitants of great cities. I see no reason to think that it was otherwise in antiquity: Epictetus has described for us the dreadful loneliness that can beset a man in the midst of his fellows. Such loneliness must have been felt by millions—the urbanised tribesman, the peasant come to town in search of work, the demobilised soldier, the rentier ruined by inflation, and the manumitted slave. For people in that situation membership of a Christian community might be the only way of maintaining their self-respect and giving their life some semblance of meaning. Within the community there was human warmth: someone was interested in them, both here and hereafter. It is therefore not surprising that the earliest and the most striking advances of Christianity were made in the great cities—in Antioch, in Rome, in Alexandria. Christians were in a more than formal sense members of one another. I think that was a major cause, perhaps the strongest single cause, of the spread of Christianity.[26]

In the early church, those who had been lost, wandering through life, restless and afraid, found a place to belong in the City of God on earth—the church. This was God's intent in creating the church. Today, our longing and need for true community has not changed. Our constant selfishness results in constant loneliness. But God has given to all who believe the gift of reconciliation—reconciliation with God through Christ and with others through the body of Christ, the church. The church is a gift from God where we find our longing and need for true community best fulfilled.

CHAPTER 4

THE CHURCH AS MOTHER

In P. D. Eastman's children's book *Are You My Mother?*,[27] a little bird, who has fallen out of his nest, goes in search of his mother. His earnest quest is met with constant disappointment and confusion as he moves from creature to creature, until he finally finds his mother. It is clear even to the smallest child that when the bird comes upon the cat or the cow or the dog and asks "Are you my mother?" he should keep looking. The underlying premise of the book is the truth that every creature has a mother.

When we become Christians, we are born again (John 3:1–8), are adopted as sons and daughters (Rom. 8:13–15), and join the spiritual family of God (1 Pet. 4:17). In this spiritual family, God is our Father and other Christians are our brothers and sisters; but who is our mother?

CHURCH AS MOTHER

Centuries ago, Cyprian, a church father from the third century, provided an answer for this question, famously saying, "No one can have God as his Father who does not have the church as his mother."[28] Augustine, a church father from the fourth century, also identified the church as our mother when he commented: "Look, mother church is in labor, see, she is groaning in travail to give birth to you ... Praise your Lord because you are being suckled, praise him; because you are being nourished, praise him; because you are being reared, advance in age."[29]

The idea that the church is the mother of Christians was not only widely affirmed in the first few centuries of Christianity,[30] it also found great traction among the Protestant Reformers. Martin Luther discusses the motherhood of the church in his comments on the Apostle's Creed in his larger catechism. He affirms that the Holy Spirit makes Christians holy through the church, "which is the mother that begets and bears every Christian through the Word of God."[31] John Calvin agreed and added:

> I will begin with the church into whose bosom God is pleased to collect his children, not only that by her aid and ministry they may be nourished so long as they are babes and children, but may also be guided by her maternal care until they grow up to manhood and, finally, attain to the perfection of fatih. What God has thus joined, let no man put asunder (Mark 10:9). To those to whom he is a Father, the church must also be a mother.[32]

Cyprian, Augustine, Luther, and Calvin all agree: the church provides Christians with the nurture, guidance, and encouragement necessary for spiritual development — most often associated with the role of a mother. But where did these church fathers and Reformers get the idea that the church is our mother? They found it in the Bible.

The Bible clearly teaches that God's people have always needed maternal care. When God gathered together the people of Israel, Moses reveals the people's need as he complains to God: "Did I conceive all these people? Did I give them birth? Why do you tell me to carry them in my arms, as a nurse carries an infant, to the land you promised on oath to their forefathers?" (Num. 11:12). When Jesus comes along, it is no surprise that he laments the spiritual condition of God's people with maternal imagery. "O Jerusalem, Jerusalem, you who kill the prophets and stone those sent to you, how often I have longed to gather your children together, as a hen gathers her chicks under her wings" (Matt. 23:37). So, too, Paul says of the church in Thessalonica: "We were gentle among you, like a mother caring for her little children" (1 Thess. 2:7); and to the churches in

Galatia he writes: "My dear children, for whom I am again in the pains of childbirth until Christ is formed in you" (Gal. 4:19).

The Bible is not only clear that Christians need maternal care to grow, but it teaches us that the church is the one who provides that care. As Paul finishes talking about his work as an apostle using maternal language in Galatians 4:19, he launches into another discussion in 4:21 – 31: "The Jerusalem that is above is free, and *she is our mother*" (4:26, italics added). As we saw in the last chapter, "the Jerusalem that is above" refers to the City of God, which is present in our time as the church, the earthly gathering of God's people.

Moreover, the apostle John writes to "the chosen lady and her children" (2 John 1, cf. v. 5), and he sends his greetings as one of the "children of your chosen sister" (2 John 13). While some interpreters believe that the "lady" in verses 1 and 5 refers to a particular woman, the view expressed by some in the ancient church, and the consensus among scholars today, is that the "lady" is the local church.[33] The members of the church are "her children" and "her sister" is the local church in Ephesus, of which John is the pastor.

Several other texts likewise infer that the church is mother, though without explicitly stating so. In Ephesians 4:11 – 16, Paul writes that God created the church and gave gifted men and women to serve in the church so that we as Christians might no longer be infants, but might grow up in every way to be a mature adult (4:14 – 15). To take an infant and transform them into a mature adult is the responsibility of parents, and since 3:14 – 15 identifies God as the Father of this family of believers, it is *implied* that the local church is the mother, who nurtures and helps God's children mature in faith.

In a similar vein, 1 Corinthians 3 begins with maternal imagery. "Brothers, I could not address you as spiritual but as worldly — mere infants in Christ. I gave you milk, not solid food, for you were not yet ready for it" (1 Cor. 3:1 – 2). The chapter goes on to speak about why Paul had expected the Corinthian Christians to be more mature: he had "planted" them in a "field" (3:8–9). This "field" is the local church at Corinth. Even though Paul switches from a maternal to an agricultural metaphor, the point is that the church is designed to provide nurturing and bring about the growth normally associated with a mother. Although Paul is the one who originally began this "maternal" ministry in Corinth, he was doing it in and through the local church.

More than that, Paul writes this letter to suggest that it is now the responsibility of the local church to continue the work of nurturing and growth. Throughout his ministry Paul has indicated that the maternal work he began as an apostle is now being transferred to the local church.[34] Such texts have led many Christians and church leaders throughout the centuries to believe that the church is a mother for Christians.

HOW IS THE CHURCH OUR MOTHER?

If the above is true, we must examine precisely how the church serves as our mother. When the Bible talks about the church as our mother, it does so most commonly in connection with the ideas of growth, nurturing, and maturation. To ask how the church is our mother is really to ask, "How does the church provide the nurture, care, and maturation for spiritual growth?" It is helpful to unpack the maternal imagery by looking more closely at how a mother helps her children grow. By better understanding the unique role of a mother, we will better understand how the church helps Christians to grow.[35]

Who Am I?

In Wendell Berry's novel *Jayber Crow*, the title character recalls the confusion he experienced upon his arrival at an orphanage after his parents and guardians had died:

> I was who? A little somebody who could have been anybody looking across that wide desk at Brother Whitespade. I knew that I could not leave until he told me to go. "Jonah Crow,"

he said, looking at a paper on his desk. And then he looked back at me. "Mr. Crow, since I believe you have not yet found your way to Ninevah, I will call you J." ... I thought at first Brother Whitespade, by changing my name to J., had made me a special case. But I soon found that all of us orphans—who were called "students"—were known by the initial letter of our first names along with our last names ... We were thus not quite nameless, but also not named. The effect was curious. For a while anyhow, and for how long a while it would be hard to say, we all acted on the assumption that we were no longer the persons we had been—which for all practical purposes was the correct assumption. We became in some way faceless to ourselves and one another.[36]

As an orphan, Jayber Crow found that he had lost his identity. All that had given him a sense of belonging—of being a *someone* in the world—was gone. One of the most important ways in which mothers help their children to grow and mature is to provide them with the gift of identity. Parents help us to know who we are, and a strong identity serves as a powerful guide as we grow and develop.

The same is true for us as Christians. Paul says, "I have been crucified with Christ and I no longer live, but Christ lives in me" (Gal. 2:20). By dying with Christ, we surrender our identity as non-Christians and receive new identities as Christians, people indwelt by the Spirit of Christ. As we identify ourselves more and more strongly with Jesus—instead of with who we used to be—we start down the path of becoming more and more like Jesus. That is why we are commanded not to conform any longer to the pattern of this world, but to be transformed in an ongoing way as our minds grasp more and more who we now are in Christ (Rom. 12:2).

One of the primary ways in which we learn to stop thinking of ourselves as we did apart from Christ and start thinking of ourselves more and more as a new creation in Christ is through participation in a local church. This is one reason why God has given the church the gifts of baptism and communion. When we are baptized, we are baptized into the body of Christ. Baptism is a sign that I have been "born again." I am a new creation in Christ. I have a new identity in Jesus. When I take communion in the church, I am reminded that I am a participant in Christ, and sharing this meal strengthens and shapes my identity. After all, how can I continue to think of myself as being "of this world" when the bread I am eating is a participation in the body of Christ and the cup that I am drinking a participation in the blood of Christ (1 Cor. 10:16)?

Even something as ordinary as regularly attending a church reminds me that I am a new creation in Christ. After all, everything in church is oreinted around Christ, not me. By choosing to participate weekly in the body of Christ, I am reminded that I have a new identity. I am not my own; I belong to Jesus.

These are some of the tangible ways in which every church helps believers know who they now are in Christ. When a mother helps her child understand who they are in this world, the child is empowered to grow and mature in accordance with who they are. When the church offers us baptism, communion, and the opportunity for regular participation, it does the work of a mother and shapes our identity.

Enduring Suffering

I love the fact that when I come home, my kids run to the door to greet me. It is fun to see them excited when I offer to play with them. I love that they want to ride in my car with me. However, there is one particular time when their desire is clearly not for me: it is when they are hurt. Or sick. Or need comfort. In these cases, they want only one person — Mom. This is true even if I have been the one playing with them or was the first one to get to them after an injury. It does not matter. Only Mom can truly bring comfort when they are suffering.

While I wish that my kids would never get hurt, be sick, or suffer, this is an unavoidable part of growing up. And one of the great things my wife brings to the table is the unique ability to comfort them as they go through these growing pains.

The same is true of church. Suffering is a necessary part of growing in the Christian faith. No one can be like Christ without experiencing suffering. It is one of the major ways that God brings about our maturity. Just as mothers are able to provide unique comfort to hurting children, so the church is able to comfort those who are growing like Christ through suffering. In Philippians 1:27 – 2:2 Paul urges the Philippian church *to strive together* as one person and not to be frightened by those who cause them to suffer through persecution. Paul promises that since he is not able to be with them in person, the comfort of Christ's love and the fellowship of the Spirit in tenderness and compassion will be with them through the church as they experience these sufferings together.

In the church in Corinth was a man who was suffering a great deal because of his sinful actions. However, he had repented, and Paul tells the church: "Now instead, you ought to forgive and comfort him, so that he will not be overwhelmed by excessive sorrow. I urge you, therefore, to reaffirm your love for him" (2 Cor. 2:7 – 8). This comfort in the midst of suffering comes through the church, just like a mother who comforts her child after having disciplined him.

Ecclesiastes says that "two are better than one," because

if one falls down,
    his friend can help him up.
But pity the man who falls
    and has no one to help him up!
Also, if two lie down together, they will keep warm.
    But how can one keep warm alone?
Though one may be overpowered,
    two can defend themselves.
A cord of three strands is not quickly broken. (Eccl. 4:9 – 12)

This is how the church is to function. God says that when one person in the church suffers, the whole church suffers with her (1 Cor. 12:26). Just as a mother feels the pain of her children — suffering when they suffer — so too the church suffers when any member of the church suffers. In this way the church is best positioned to offer motherly comfort to those who are in the midst of suffering so that they might endure and grow as a result.

Feeding the Hungry Mouths

Mothers are also responsible for feeding their hungry children. After all, how can babies grow if they are not fed? When the Bible talks about the Word of God, it often uses the metaphor of food. Infant's milk and solid food (Heb. 5:12–13), bread (Matt. 4:4), and honey (Ps. 19:9–10) are all used to help us recognize the nourishing character of the Word of God. Likewise, the Lord's Supper is pictured as nourishment for the growing Christian. The bread and the cup signify the life-sustaining power that comes from fellowship with Jesus.

If the Word of God and the Lord's Supper are two primary means by which Christians are nourished in their spiritual walk, it is clear that God intends to provide this nourishment to us through the local church. The gatherings of the early New Testament church are described as being centered around the apostles' teachings and the breaking of bread (the Lord's Supper; see Acts 2:42, 46). God gives to the local church spiritually gifted believers, many of whom have gifts oriented around the proclamation and teaching of the Word of God. He instructs those who participate in local churches to bring a word of instruction to their worship services (1 Cor. 14:26). He has also entrusted the celebration of the Lord's Supper to local churches. Just as a mother provides food for her children to grow, the church nourishes all who participate in it.

Imitating a Godly Example

James McBride has written a beautiful book about his mother and her Christian faith, entitled *The Color of Water: A Black Man's*

Tribute to His White Mother.[37] One thing becomes clear as James narrates not only his mother's story but also his own: Although there were struggles along the way, James ends up adopting his mother's moral orientation toward life. This is not suprising. One of the key factors for growth in children is modeling appropriate behavior for them. The field of social psychology is replete with findings that suggest children learn what their parents model for them. In particular, studies have shown that the morality of children is often closely connected to the morality of their mothers.[38]

This is true not only in familial relationships, but also in spiritual relationships. Jesus called disciples to himself and urged them to follow his example (John 13:15–17). Paul regularly told those in his churches to imitate him (1 Cor. 11:1; Phil. 3:17). He exhorted the church leaders to set an example and encouraged believers to walk in the way of their leaders (1 Cor. 4:16–17; 1 Tim. 4:12; Titus 2:7). We become more like Christ as we imitate his example and the example of more mature Christians. While we can find the example of Jesus recorded in Scripture, it is in the local church that we can find mature believers to imitate today.

Titus 2:4 says that older women in the church are to train younger women to love their husbands and children. Many churches use a mentoring program called *Apples of Gold* to help with this process of training and mentoring. Through this program older women in the church fulfill Titus 2:4 by using cooking classes and meal planning as a means to share love, advice, wisdom, and life experiences with younger women. It is God's intention for the church to serve as a mother by being the place we find godly examples to imitate.

Discipline

One of the most trying aspects of being a mother deals with is discipline. No parent enjoys correcting and training a child, yet discipline is essential for every child to grow and mature. So, too, discipline is necessary for us to grow as Christians. Hebrews 12 tells us that God as our Father disciplines us for our holiness. If he did not, he would not be much of a father.

While God as our Father directly disciplines wayward Christians, he has also entrusted a major part of the discipline process to the local church. Acts 5:1–11 is the first recorded act of Christian discipline—and it happened in the context of a local church gathering. According to Matthew 18:15–20, when someone sins against you, you must show him his fault. If he does not listen, you are to take two or three others with you. If he refuses to listen to them, the matter is to be turned over to church. If the sinning brother refuses to listen to the church, the church is to exercise church discipline by severing fellowship with the sinning brother until he repents.

In 1 Corinthians 5 Paul writes that if someone who calls himself a brother continues in blatant and unrepentant sinful behavior, the local church is to remove that person from the fellowship of the church and turn him over to Satan. (By the way—if the local church is *not* a gift from God, why would taking it away from a sinning Christian be considered discipline? Clearly, God sees his church as a gift, even when we do not.) The church, like a good mother, disciplines us when we wander into sin or live in disobedience to God so that we may continue to grow in holiness and become mature in our faith.

Seeing God

There is one final, yet important way in which the church enables us to grow, though it has no parallel to our human analogy of mothers and their children. The apostle Paul tells us that "we, who with unveiled faces all contemplate[39] the Lord's glory, are being transformed into his likeness with ever-increasing glory, which comes from the Lord, who is the Spirit" (2 Cor. 3:18). As we experience the Lord's presence, we grow in conformity to his image and become more like him.

This is different than consciously or subconsciously imitating the behavior of other Christians who model godly behavior for us. Something unparalleled happens when we experience Jesus directly. As we saw in chapter 2, to see Jesus is to become like him, and we see Jesus most powerfully in the local church. As we gather together in worship, Jesus' presence by his Spirit actually transforms and shapes us into the people God wants us to become.

MOTHER CHURCH

I hope you as a Christian are beginning to embrace the idea that the church is your spiritual mother. God gives us the church to help us form our identity as Christians. The church helps us to endure suffering, bringing comfort and encouragement in difficult times. The church nourishes us with the Word and the Lord's Supper, provides godly examples for us to imitate, and disciplines us when we go astray. In addition, we grow and are transformed as Jesus is uniquely manifested in our worship assemblies. The church provides maternal care for us in all of these ways, helping us to grow to become more like Jesus.

But some may object at this point: Doesn't every kind of Christian group provide some level of growth and development for its members? Can't one find godly examples to imitate outside the local church? Isn't it possible to receive good teaching from God's Word without being part of a local church? Why should we call *the church* our mother? What makes the church unique in providing these blessings and benefits?

Breast Milk or Formula?

Consider the difference between breast milk and baby formula. Thousands of hours of research and billions of dollars have been devoted to developing a substitute for breast milk. Yet, despite all of the scientific prowess and intellectual fire power that has gone into this endeavor, humans have been unable to replicate the unique advantages of breast milk for feeding infants. All other things being equal, breast milk still remains the best choice for babies.

Or consider the institution of motherhood itself. Governments and societies have attempted to replicate the institution of motherhood with humanly devised solutions like orphanages or by providing "house mothers" at boarding schools. As wonderful as these institutions are for those who lack a mother, we all know that orphanages and boarding schools cannot replace a mother. Since human beings have not been able to design adequate replacements for the things that God has originally designed (breast milk and motherhood), what is the likelihood that we as humans are able to design a replacement for the spiritual nurturing God created the church to provide?

Two Years of Formula

While I was in seminary, our school had a big push to develop "spiritual formation groups." These small groups were responsible for helping facilitate the spiritual formation of seminary students, who were required to participate. The school had become concerned that many of its graduates were full of knowledge but lacking in spiritual maturity. In the two years my wife and I participated, our group attempted to encourage one another to live out our Christian faith. We discussed important spiritual theology; we prayed together; we served together; we socialized. These spiritual formation groups were an improvement over the time in which spiritual formation was less emphasized. However, they could not replicate or replace what God has designed into the church.

We noted above that the church helps form our identity as Christ-followers through the gift of baptism, our participation in the body of Christ, and our regular celebration of the Lord's Supper. These spiritual formation groups were unable to truly form our identities as Christ-followers, first because we celebrated neither the Lord Supper nor baptism together; and second, because they strengthened our identity as seminary students as much as they formed our identity as Christians. For example, when we were in our group, we talked as much about seminary and being seminary students as we did about Christ and being Christians. As a result, we left each session reminded that we were seminary students and thinking of ourselves in those terms.

Though we offered sympathy to each other in times of trouble, as twentysomething seminary students we found we were ill-equipped to truly shepherd one another through the storms of life. We attempted to feed each other spiritually, but we could not provide the nourishment offered in church through the preached Word and the Lord's Supper. In addition, the church helps us to grow through discipline and accountability to church leaders. While spiritual formation groups provide some level of accountability, they could not exercise adequate discipline. And while a few spiritual formation groups were led by more mature professors, most groups were comprised of students of roughly the same spiritual maturity. We were the blind leading the blind, so to speak.

To be fair, these spiritual formation groups were not intended to replace the local church, though they did exactly that for several of the students not attending a local church. It was clear to many that these groups were ill-equipped for the task of nourishing and nurturing Christians to maturity. They were simply one piece of a larger puzzle. Certainly, these groups could have added baptism, communion, church discipline, and the preaching and teaching of the Scriptures. They could have provided mature Christian examples to imitate and gathered worship assemblies in which God was present. But if we had added all of these to our gatherings, we wouldn't have been a spiritual formation group any longer; we would have essentially been a local church!

WHY DOES SO MUCH IMMATURITY PERSIST IN THE LOCAL CHURCH?

Sadly, any argument for the church as an agent of growth must deal with the indisputable fact that there are those who participate regularly in church who do not seem to be growing. Why not? There are at least four reasons.

Undoubtedly, some churchgoers do not grow because *their churches are not functioning properly*. The church they attend does not truly provide the benefits that God intends the church to provide.

Second, some believers attend a healthy church, but *they do not really engage in the life of the church*. A child cannot become mature if he or she is absent from his family most of the time. Children will not become mature if they continually hop from family to family based on which mother they like the best. Unfortunately, American Christianity is rife with those who attend church but are not engaged.

Third, some people who attend a local church are not growing in the faith *because they are not actually true believers*. There are many who religiously attend church services, week after week, and may even be involved in programs and Bible studies, but they have never had a personal encounter with Jesus Christ.

There is a fourth reason, however, that is worth deeper consideration. *It may be that for many, the growth is happening, slowly and, at times, imperceptibly.* Is there any parent in the world who does not occasionally wonder if their children are maturing at all? You teach them to use the potty, and then they have a series of accidents. You help them learn from poor dating choices, only to see them make another bad choice. You teach them the importance of being a good steward only to see them blow all their money on something frivolous.

There are times, as a parent, when there seems to be no growth in a child's life at all. But then, when we step back and look at the big picture, seeing where our children have come from, we cannot help but notice that growth really is happening — slowly! Often times our children are listening even when we thought they were not. For many of us who are parents, growth does not happen as fast or as easily as we would have liked, but it is happening.

Is there a more inefficient job in all the world than being a mother? The return on investment is often painfully low. Day after

day, sweeping the same floors, reading the same books, and prob-
ing for information about how school went in an attempt to raise
godly, mature, successful children can seem as efficient as carving
Mount Rushmore with a toothpick. If we were to judge simply by
outward appearances, it would seem that camp directors are much
more effective at transforming the lives of children and youth than
mothers. Many are the stories of children who show up to camp
frightened and uninterested, only to leave a week or two later with
new friends and new ambitions — often professing a life-changing
experience at camp. Perhaps we should consider a massive layoff of
mothers and just send our kids off to camp.

Before you take me seriously, let's admit that in some ways
the mothering process is, indeed, terribly "inefficient" if we are
simply looking for quick results. But it is precisely because the
process is slow and lengthy that real change occurs. Camp has
its place — that one-week, mountaintop experience that is part of
longer-term transformation — but it isn't a model for raising children. Character is developed and lives are molded and shaped by
the "slow and steady" progress of nurturing that occurs day in and
day out. This is what gives motherhood (and parenting in general)
the power to bring about authentic change that leads to maturity.

The same is true of church. Making disciples takes time; it
doesn't happen overnight! Because churches spend so much of
their time dealing with "mundane" activities like hospital visitation, prayer meetings, weekly services, and providing nursery
care, it is sometimes easy to miss the cumulative effect that these
simple activities can have in transforming people into the image
of Christ. Weekend conferences, like a summer camp experience, can seem to have a far greater impact on a person's life than
regular, weekly participation in a small group at church. But we
shouldn't be fooled into thinking that weekend conferences are a
good way to raise Christians. Women's retreats, college seminars,
and marriage conferences all have their place — and God often
uses them to jump-start a process of spiritual transformation —

but it is the "slow and steady" process of commitment to a local church that wins the race, so to speak.

HAPPY MOTHER'S DAY!

Earlier in this chapter, we looked at a passage from a novel by Wendell Berry where he describes the loss of identity that the main character, Jayber Crow, experienced when he came to stay at an orphanage after the loss of his parents. At the conclusion of his time in the orphanage, we learn who Jayber Crow has become — his old identity has been lost and he is now a lonely orphan: "I was a scantling boy, scared and out of place and (as I now see it) odd. Not just lonely, but solitary, living as much as I could in secret, looking about, seeing much, revealing little."[40]

Berry's description of Jayber Crow also describes many Christians today who have abandoned the gift that God has given them in the local church. These Christians have rejected the mother God has provided for them, to nurture and guide them to maturity in Christ. God did not intend for his children to live out solitary, individualistic lives. God did not intend us to live in spiritual orphanages, wandering the streets of this world alone. He has given us the priceless gift of a mother: a community where we can be who we are, a place where we can be changed into who we need to be. The church is a place where we can be loved, encouraged, and corrected, where the mundane facilitates the supernatural and we are transformed from children to adults.

Every Mother's Day we stop and give thanks to God that he has provided us with mothers to love us, care for us, and help us become mature adults. But we must never forget that God has also provided each of his spiritual children with a spiritual mother to nurture us and care for us and to help us to become mature Christians. Thanks be to God that we are not left as orphans! God has given us a mother: the local church.

CHAPTER 5

MUTUAL FUNDS, X-MEN, AND THE CHURCH

Josh and Shelly were a young couple involved in the ministry of a local church. Josh had left a position at a large church because he felt burdened to reach young adults more effectively, and he and his brother-in-law had recently started a new church in the arts district of a Midwestern city. Tragically, on his first day on the job, Josh received news from his wife that a fan had fallen over, killing their youngest child, Eva. Emotionally overwhelmed with their grief, Josh and Shelly labored to make it through the pain of their loss, one day at a time.

God was faithful to this young couple, and after several difficult months, the stifling cloud of their grief began to lift. To help refresh and restore their wounded hearts, a Christian friend offered the couple a place in Mexico where they could get away for a time and reconnect as a couple. Again, however, tragedy struck unexpectedly. While they were out swimming in the ocean, a large wave slammed Josh into the ocean bed at a dangerous angle, breaking his neck. Though he survived, Josh was confined to a wheelchair as a paraplegic, and he and his wife arrived home from Mexico devastated once again.

On top of the additional care required for Josh, the couple also had two small children at home to take care of—one with special needs—and they were expecting again—a third child! Their house was not handicap accessible, creating additional difficulties for Josh. Already struggling financially and facing a mountain of medical bills, Josh and Shelly were in dire straits. They desperately needed some help. They applied to shows like *Extreme Home Makeover* and *Oprah* for help, but received nothing.

Once again, though, help came through the blessing of the church. God brought together a coalition of churches to raise money and build a house for Josh and Shelly. God made it clear that it was not the responsibility of corporate America or the government to care for the needs of this family; rather, it was the job of the church. In one of the churches that came alongside this young couple there was a little five-year-old boy named Charlie. Charlie had his own set of struggles. He was deaf in one ear and needed a hearing aid to help him in school. However, when he heard the story of Josh and Shelly, Charlie felt a clear call to do whatever he could to help them. At first, Charlie tried talking his parents into selling their house to help Josh and Shelly, but his parents reminded him that they, too, needed a place to live! Instead, Charlie decided to hold a garage sale and sold most of his toys. He also went around from house to house, collecting pop cans to raise money. He even decided to donate the money he had set aside for his own hearing aid. When the day came for collecting all the funds for Josh and Shelly, Charlie gave what God had told him to give. God used Charlie's sacrificial gift along with the donations of thousands of others, to provide not only a brand-new house for Josh and Shelly but to also buy a state-of-the-art wheelchair.

Charlie's gift, as wonderful as it was, could never have bought a house. But since Charlie gave in faith and his gift was combined with thousands of other gifts from others in the church, it was multiplied far beyond his own abilities. There is an old African proverb that says: "He who goes alone, goes faster; but those who go together, go farther." In this chapter I'd like to share with you a key reason why the church is a gift from God: that together as the body of Christ we can go farther and accomplish far more than we could ever do on our own as individuals. The church is a God-designed means of multiplying ministry to those in need.

MUTUAL FUNDS, X-MEN, AND THE CHURCH

Mutual funds are common investments for those planning their future retirement. The principle behind a mutual fund is simple: better returns can be found when money is pooled and invested together. So, for example, an investor that has $500 may not be able to invest in a single share of a particular stock, and she certainly cannot diversify her portfolio. However, if she invests in a mutual fund, her $500 will be combined with the investments of other people, now making it possible for her $500 to be invested in a variety of different companies. Her mutual fund investments also have the added benefit of a fund manager who has expertise, experience, and time devoted to investing—far beyond her meager abilities and opportunities.

We find something similar in the world of comic books. In 1963, comic book geniuses Stan Lee and Jack Kirby, working for Marvel Comics, introduced a new set of heroes called the X-Men. The X-Men have since become one of the most popular comic book franchises in the world. There are now several hit movies, television shows, and even video games and books based on these characters. The story that underlies the X-Men franchise is the idea that some humans have been born with mutant superpowers. Isolated and untrained, these mutants pose a significant threat to themselves and to the world. Yet together, working under the leadership of Professor Charles Xavier, these same mutants can actually become a force for good, using their powers to work together for peace. The X-Men succeed by blending their diverse abilities together under the tutelage of their leader. Working together, they are able to accomplish far more than they could on their own as individuals.

It's not a controversial idea: *together we can accomplish more than we can as individuals.* We all recognize the value of teamwork, of partnerships, of working together with others who have skills and abilities that we lack. But have you ever considered that this is one of the main reasons why God has given us the church?

QUANTITATIVELY AND QUALITATIVELY MORE

Mutual funds enable *quantitatively* more to happen. If one person contributes $500 to an investment project, there is $500. If ten people contribute $500, there is now $5,000, which is *quantitatively* more than $500. The X-Men, on the other hand, are able to do *qualitatively* more when they work together. The X-Men would not be much of a team if every X-Man had the same powers. But because some can fly, some have superstrength, some have telekinetic powers, and so on, together they are able to do *qualitatively* more than they could separately.

The church enables us to do more by working together than we could accomplish individually. This is true both *quantitatively* and *qualitatively*. When we all come together and each person gives of their time, talent, and treasure as prompted by God, there is certainly a greater quantity of resources available to do kingdom work. In the early days of Christianity, the church in Jerusalem was experiencing a major famine and had great financial needs. To bring relief to these struggling Christians, Paul went to the churches he had planted and asked them to save up their money to assist their fellow Christians in Jerusalem (see 1 Cor. 16:1–2; 2 Cor. 8–9). This collection of funds was then taken to Jerusalem to provide for the material needs of the Christians living there. Believers living in Corinth, Galatia, and Philippi were able to do more quantitatively by pooling their resources together to serve their brothers and sisters in Christ.

The church also enables us to do qualitatively more. Imagine you have $20 that you want to give to help those who are in financial need. You could find someone who looks like they need that $20 and give it to them. Or you could give that $20 to a church to use in their benevolence ministry. Our church does not give out cash. Instead, we give away vouchers we have purchased—usually at a discount—from prescreened restaurants, hotels, taxis, gas stations, psychological counselors, and grocery stores, or we arrange to make payments on mortgage or utility bills. The people who need help are entered into a citywide database. We also take them through an assessment process to see what other needs they might have, whether for budget counseling, spiritual guidance, employment issues, help with substance abuse, or domestic abuse. A group of people from the church prays constantly for those involved. We share the gospel when appropriate as well as try to incorporate those who are Christians into a church family. When I give my $20 to this benevolence ministry, it is combined with the gifts, talents, experiences, and efforts of others to provide qualitatively more for those in need than simply handing such people a small amount of cash.

There are three primary reasons why we are able to accomplish more through the church:

- God has given the church a diversity of *spiritual gifts*, which function together to accomplish the mission he has assigned us.
- God has given the church *specific leaders* to oversee the work.
- God has given the church *special access* to divine power.

Each of these reasons helps us to better understand how God multiplies the work of ministry through the gift of the local church.

REASON 1: SPIRITUAL GIFTS — A GREAT RECIPE!

As a part of the blessing of diversity, God gives us a wide variety of spiritual gifts to accomplish the mission that Jesus has given us. Spiritual gifts are supernatural empowerments given by the Holy Spirit. With them we are able to teach, encourage, give, show mercy, offer wisdom to others, and do many other activities in the power of the Holy Spirit. Every Christian is given at least one spiritual gift, and no Christian has received the full range of such gifts.

The Bible uses the image of a "body" when describing spiritually gifted Christians (1 Cor. 12:12–27). Each Christian who has been endowed with a spiritual gift is like a part of the body.

Some are like the eyes, others are like ears, and still others are like the hands and feet. Every part of the body, like every spiritual gift, serves a different purpose and has a different role and function. Just as God has designed our physical bodies with appropriate members, he has also arranged each part of Christ's spiritual body—the church—just as he desires so that the ministry and the work we do are multiplied.

Because the Bible uses the image of body, it is the best analogy to consider. But I have also found another metaphor that helps me see the idea of spiritual gifts from a different angle. I like to think of the mix of spiritual gifts in the church somewhat like the process of baking a cake. To properly bake, you need a variety of different ingredients: eggs, flour, salt, sugar, milk, oil, and baking soda. These different ingredients are mixed together, and in the process of mixing them the unique properties of each ingredient combine with the other ingredients to create something new. A cake is not just a stack of eggs covered in a pile of flour and a mound of sugar. It is a cake—a mixture of these individual ingredients, baked together to become something new (and quite delicious). This is similar to God's purpose for his church. He takes individuals with different spiritual gifts, mixes them together, and "bakes" them under the fire of his Spirit, until they become something more than they were as individuals—qualitatively and quantitatively.

God is the master baker, and he provides all of the ingredients for the cake just as he sees fit. God promises to provide the right mix of teachers, encouragers, administrators, helpers, and whoever else is needed for the church to accomplish whatever it is that he intends for it to do. God does not give his gifts to some churches and withhold them from others. Specific material resources may vary from church to church, but God is the one who oversees the distribution of the gifts of the Spirit, making sure that each church has the full complement of spiritual gifts. Each local church is called the body of Christ (1 Cor. 12:27), which implies that every local church will have *all* the parts of the body that are needed—arms, feet, hands, eyes, and ears—with each part representing a different spiritual gift.

Using our new metaphor, each local church is also its own "cake." You can't bake a cake if you are missing some of the ingredients. But God promises each local church that they will have all the spiritual ingredients necessary to do the complete mission of God. Even a church the size of Corinth (likely around thirty to ninety people at the time of Paul's writing)[41] is said to possess the *full* range of spiritual gifts (1 Cor. 1:7).

Keep in mind that these promises are given to the local church, not to small groups of Christians or travelling bands of evangelists. There are no promises that guarantee the full range of gifts for those involved in ministries apart from a local church. Our modern-day parachurch ministries, as helpful as they can be for accomplishing specific ministries, are not truly representations of *the* body of Christ; rather, they are simply a collection of parts of the body of Christ—a group of arms or legs from the body of the larger church. A body will always be able to accomplish more than a group of arms or legs can accomplish alone. Parachurch ministries are still serving a useful function in the kingdom of God, but need to be integrated with a local church to fully maximize their potential.

Or imagine a family that believes they can raise their children to spiritual maturity apart from the local church.[42] Children—both those who are young of age and those who are young in faith—need exposure to the full range of spiritual gifts to mature and grow to be like Christ. Parents will certainly have particular gifts of the Spirit, but they will not be gifted in every way (1 Cor. 12:29–31). Without a church community, how will children be exposed to all the spiritually empowered wisdom, teaching, encouragement, and mercy that they need? Children whose parents are not gifted as teachers, for example, will miss out on the grace of God that is available to them through spiritually gifted teachers in the local church.

Some parents might be inclined to believe that books, internet sermons, and Bible classes at a Christian school will meet those needs. But again we must recognize the truth that a cake is more than a collection of ingredients. If you eat two cups of flour, digest some eggs, and drink some milk, you have not eaten a "cake." Only when those ingredients are mixed together and baked at the right temperature for the right time do they become a cake. Church is where God intends the mixing and baking to occur, for the right time, at the right temperature, through the unique work of his Spirit among the gathered body of believers.

REASON 2: LEADERS — "WITHOUT ITS HEAD, A SNAKE IS ONLY A ROPE"

Another passage of Scripture relevant to the discussion of spiritual gifts is Ephesians 4. When Paul speaks in this chapter of Jesus giving gifts to his church, the gifts he refers to are not functional abilities. Rather, they are *people*—leaders for the church. This is the second way in which the church enables us to accomplish more together and thus multiplying our individual ministries. God gives leaders to his church.

Another African proverb that I appreciate says that "without its head, a snake is only a rope." In other words: leaders are essential to the success of communities. The Bible makes this same point using a somewhat different metaphor. When Moses, facing his own death, prays that God will provide a leader for Israel in his coming absence, he prays for this leader so that the people will not become "like sheep without a shepherd" (Num. 27:17). This metaphor, referring to leaders of God's people as shepherds, recurs throughout the Old Testament (e.g., 1 Kings 22:17; Ezek. 34:5–6; Zech. 10:2). Unfortunately, since most of us no longer live in an agrarian culture, the emotional impact of this metaphor is sometimes lost on us today.

Think, for example, of a leaderless community as a classroom without a teacher, a football team without a quarterback, a committee without a chairperson, a legal team without lead counsel, or a tour group without a guide (or the X-Men without Professor Xavier). In each example, the point is the same: a leaderless group will never accomplish much of value. Conversely, the church is able to accomplish more because God has given the church specific people who lead—shepherds for the sheep.

Shepherds after My Own Heart

Throughout the Old Testament, the leaders of God's people failed time after time. Pained by the failure of these leaders, God made a solemn promise to his people in Jeremiah 3:15: "I will give you shepherds after my own heart, who will lead you with knowledge and understanding." Jesus is the clear fulfillment of this promise, a leader after God's own heart. We read in Matthew 9:36 that Jesus cared for God's people and "had compassion on them, because they were harassed and helpless, like sheep without a shepherd." But Jesus, the Great Shepherd of his people (Matt. 26:31; John 10; Heb. 13:20; 1 Pet. 2:25; Rev. 7:17), is simply first in a line of shepherds who would fulfill the promise of Jeremiah 3:15.

As Jesus was preparing to ascend to heaven, he assigned to Peter the task of being a shepherd serving Jesus' sheep (John 21:15–17). When Ephesians 4 lists gifted leaders Jesus gives to the church, one of those is the "pastor"—an English translation of the Greek word for "shepherd" (Eph. 4:11). In 1 Peter 5:1–4, God commands elders in the church to serve as faithful shepherds under the authority of Jesus. Jesus, the Chief Shepherd, now gives shepherds to his churches in his absence so that his church might accomplish its mission. The witness of the book of Acts confirms that God was fulfilling his promise of Jeremiah 3 by providing leadership for the church from its very infancy (Acts 1:12–26; 13:1–2; 20:28).

This pattern continued long after the era narrated in the New Testament Scriptures.[43] Christians in the early church recognized their leaders were gifts from God, given to build up, equip, and

train the body of Christ for greater effectiveness and faithful-
ness to God's mission. God continues to fulfill the promise of
Jeremiah 3:15 today by providing shepherds after his own heart
to lead his people, bringing them together in unity to serve God's
purposes in our generation. Good leaders multiply the impact of
the gifted body by training individuals in the use of their gifts
and discerning the best way to utilize those gifts in partnership
together.

But Aren't We All Leaders?

Some today object to the idea of "leaders" in the church—that
is, the idea that some people hold positions where they can give
direction and oversight to the rest of the body. Perhaps they are
simply echoing the sentiments of those who challenged Moses in
Numbers 16:3 saying, "The whole community is holy, every one of
them, and the LORD is with them. Why then do you set yourselves
above the LORD's assembly?" Or perhaps they object to the idea
of a "privileged" position, much like the objection of Moses' own
sister and brother in Numbers 12:2: "Has the LORD spoken only
through Moses?... Hasn't he also spoken through us?" In both
cases, God appeared and made it clear that while we are all equal
before him, there are some (like Moses) who hold a unique position of leadership—and that this is actually good for the people!

Sometimes good ideas have bad consequences. In the 1500s,
during the Reformation, Martin Luther argued vigorously that
every believer is also a minister. As wonderful as this truth is
(a doctrine commonly known as the priesthood of all believers),
taken too far it can have unintended consequences. Even among
a priesthood of all believers some are still called out to serve as
leaders for the church. In his own day, Luther saw some beginning
to despise leadership in the church, and he was horrified by it. In
response to the "devaluing" of ordained ministry, Luther wrote "A
Sermon on Keeping Children in School," in which he argued that
there is an ongoing need for certain individuals to be set apart as

leaders in the church. Luther quotes John 14:12 in his sermon: "Anyone who has faith in me will do what I have been doing. He will do even greater things than these." He goes on to comment:

> If the single believer can accomplish these things working independently with individuals, how much more will the preacher accomplish working publicly with the whole company of people? It is not the man, though, that does it. It is his office, ordained by God for this purpose. That is what does it—that and the word of God which he teaches. He is only the instrument through which it is accomplished.[44]

Luther fiercely defended the biblical doctrine that every Christian is called to serve God as a minister of the gospel, but he defended with equal fervor the idea that God sets apart gifted leaders to model, guide, and direct that ministry.

All Too Human

But aren't human leaders in the church the *cause* of so many problems? How can they be one of the means by which God enables us to accomplish more? One of the mysterious things about God is that he often chooses to work through human beings when he could seemingly do much better without us. Theologian Timothy Laniak, commenting on this unusual partnership, writes: "The God of Scripture passionately seeks humans to enlist in his mission, risking it regularly in their hands ... Our theology of leadership is informed by this breathtaking choice of God to grant royal prerogatives to his creatures."[45]

Unfortunately, one of the realities of God's choosing to use human leaders is that these leaders can easily abuse their position. God commands that his shepherds search for the lost, bind the injured, strengthen the weak, lead the sheep beside still waters, and shepherd with justice. But Jude 12 warns us that there will always be leaders in the church who are selfish and care little for the people under their care — "shepherds who feed only themselves." Eugene Petersen, an author and pastor, admits that leaders in the church will inevitably face the temptation of abusing their position for selfish gain:

> A large part of my identity comes in relation to the way my congregation is perceived by others ... As I get people working with me, my image is enhanced. And in the course of doing this, I cross a line: what started out as managing people's gifts for the work of the kingdom of God becomes the manipulation of people's lives for the building up of my pastoral ego.[46]

While Peterson's candid confession and awareness of the temptation is refreshing, far too many leaders in the church remain blissfully unaware when we make the subtle shift from *serving* others to *using* others.

Despite the failings of leaders in the church, God has promised to care for the needs of his people by giving them godly leaders, shepherds after his own heart. When I was an intern at the church where I currently serve as senior pastor, Ed Dobson, senior pastor at the time, came by my office and asked if I wanted to make a hospital visit with him. I readily agreed to go. On the way out the door, I asked, "Who are we visiting?" "A man with ALS," was Ed's reply.[47] I was caught off guard for a moment. Ed had himself been recently diagnosed with ALS, and I had watched him suffer through the pain and sorrow of that diagnosis. I wasn't sure what our visit would entail.

When we arrived at the hospital room, we found a man hooked up to a machine. His hand, when I touched it, was cold and lifeless. At this stage of the disease, he was only able to move his eyebrow; the rest of his body was immobilized. A computer had been hooked up that allowed him to "type" sentences and communicate with others by raising and lowering his eyebrow. I remember sitting there for a long time while Ed talked with the man. Through his computer the man shared with us that his wife had recently divorced him because she was tired of waiting for him to die. Alone in this hospital room, he was slowly becoming trapped within his own lifeless body. It was a horrifying situation, and devastatingly sad for me to watch.

I managed to hold my emotions in check while we sat with the man, but after we left, I was overcome with sorrow. I sobbed and sobbed. Regaining my composure, I said to Ed, "I would never wish that on anyone, not even on my worst enemy." Before I had even finished speaking, I suddenly realized that Ed was crying as well: this was his disease, and barring a miracle, his future. Why would he choose to visit someone with the same disease? Didn't he find that discouraging?

When I got up the courage, I asked him why he had come. Ed said there were two reasons. First, this man needed to be cared for, and there was nobody able to understand his situation better than a fellow ALS sufferer. Perhaps, he said to me, this was the very reason that God had allowed him to be afflicted with ALS. Second, Ed knew that as a pastor, he couldn't be honest and encourage those of us under his care to face potentially difficult futures if he wasn't willing to face his own. His decision to visit this man was motivated by compassion and a deep sense of personal integrity. Ed Dobson's motto was simple: "Preach the word and love people," and he is well-known for doing both.[48] Through the example of his leadership that day, I realized what a gift godly pastoral leaders are for the church.

Pastors versus Presidents and Deacons versus Directors

The church is not unique in having leaders. We find leaders in every segment of society—politics, business, sports, school, and family. So what makes the leadership of the church any different than the type of leadership we find in other segments of society? Why are leaders in the church a unique gift to God's people?

Certainly, godly leaders are a blessing to any group. We are grateful for leaders who honor God while leading a business or serving in government. But the leaders whom God gives to the church are differentiated by four key characteristics:

First, God says he will give to the church shepherds who will lead with *godly motives.* They will lead by example and not fiat; they will serve out of love for the Lord, not personal gain; they will be filled with the Holy Spirit and wisdom, not selfish ambition and a drive for personal advancement. Church leaders are servants of Christ, not executives, treasurers, dictators, generals, provosts, or trustees (see 1 Pet. 5:1–4).

Second, God has much *higher qualifications* for those who will lead in the church. Many institutions look for leaders who have a certain education or possess a particular charisma, and sadly that is still true of many churches. But the qualifications for church leadership given in the Bible are much more demanding. God asks that leaders for the church be self-controlled, gentle, and hospitable (1 Tim. 3; Titus 1:5–9). I am personally familiar with a man at another church who runs his own company, is on the board of several Christian organizations, leads Bible studies, chairs committees, and has even worked on the staff of a Christian ministry. While he has done many things well to serve the cause of Christ, he is not qualified to be an elder in the church because he consistently fails one of the tests of Christian character in Titus 1. Although he can certainly lead these other ministries, God requires the leaders of his church to exhibit a consistently higher level of godly character.[49]

Third, when God gives leaders to the church, he gives them a *spiritual endowment* that enables them to lead his people (1 Tim. 4:14). Leaders who are set apart and called to serve the body of Christ are also uniquely empowered by God's Spirit to fulfill the responsibilities of their calling. As they preach and teach, counsel, and care for the church, they do so in the power that God provides for the building up of the body of Christ.

Finally, when God places a leader in a church, that person *assumes a position* in a line of ministers that stretches back to the apostles commissioned by Jesus. As a result, church leaders are not free to reinvent their responsibilities or the nature of their calling. They are constrained by the teaching of Scripture and the example of those who have gone before them as to what they can believe and teach. There are patterns of ministry to which they must conform. These connections to Christ and others are a blessing both to the leader and the church.

REASON 3: SPECIAL ACCESS TO GOD'S POWER — MORE THAN NATURAL

James 5:14–15 says, "Is any one of you sick? He should call the elders of the church to pray over him and anoint him with oil in the name of the Lord. And the prayer offered in faith will make the sick person well; the Lord will raise him up. If he has sinned, he will be forgiven." It is significant that God does not tell us to call our doctors, our Bible study leaders, our friends, or our spouses. He says specifically to "call the elders of the church." Why? God has given the local church unique access to his power, and these leaders are able to draw on that supernatural power to accomplish miraculous things. As we mentioned earlier, one of the benefits to investing in a mutual fund is that the mutual fund manager has access to information, research, and analysis that the average investor does not have the opportunity to obtain. The same is true of the church.

Second Kings 5 tells the story of Naaman the Syrian, a man who desperately wanted to be healed of leprosy. His wife's servant happened to be an Israelite girl, and she urged Namaan to seek healing in Israel, from the God of Israel. So Naaman went to his master, the king of Syria, and asked him to write a letter to the king of Israel, requesting help and healing. The king of Syria, pleased with his servant, Naaman, wrote the letter. But when the king of Israel received the request, he was overwhelmed. He responded back to the king of Syria with exasperatation: "Am I God? Can I kill and bring back to life? Why does this fellow send someone to me to be cured of his leprosy?" (2 Kings 5:7). The king of Israel knew that he had no ability to heal Naaman.

But Elisha the prophet heard about this unusual request and told the king that the man should come to him for healing. When Naaman came to see Elisha, Elisha gave him one simple instruction: wash in the Jordan River seven times. When Naaman heard these instructions, he was angry: "I thought that he would surely come out to me and stand and call on the name of the LORD his God, wave his hand over the spot and cure me of my leprosy. Are not Abana and Pharpar, the rivers of Damascus, better than any of the waters of Israel? Couldn't I wash in them and be cleansed?" (2 Kings 5:11–12). Naaman was filled with pride, cynicism, and anger, yet despite his frustration, he knew this was his best hope of being healed. He obeyed Elisha's instruction, even though it made no sense to him at the time. He was healed of his leprosy.

We can draw two insights from this story as we consider the role of the church and God's power to heal. First, God healed through his *anointed representative*, Elisha, the man of God; he was the only one who could offer the healing of God. Second, healing came through *faith expressing itself in obedience,* even when what was being asked didn't make much sense, at least from a human perspective. The rivers in Damascus probably were cleaner that the Jordan River, but they were not the way that God had chosen to heal Naaman.

When God tells us to call the elders of the church to pray for healing, he is saying that we are to call his *appointed representatives*, who are found in the local church. When we do so, we are exercising faith through obedience — despite what our own wisdom tells us. This is the faith that brings the healing power of God into our lives. Even those who are skeptical about the church, when faced with a life-threatening illness, should realize to themselves as Naaman did, that their best chance for healing is to obey God. While God does encourage us to use medicine (see 1 Tim. 5:23, for example) and does heal that way, he has granted his church and its leaders, like the prophets of the Old Testament, unique access to his supernatural healing power.

The encouragement to call the elders of the church when you and I are sick builds on what Jesus himself said of the local church: "Whatever you [the church] bind on earth will be bound in heaven, and whatever you loose on earth will be loosed in heaven. Again, I tell you that if two of you on earth agree about anything you ask for, it will be done for you by my Father in heaven" (Matt. 18:18–19). The church has been given special access to the power and authority of God through the work of Jesus Christ. A parallel passage in 1 Corinthians says something similar: "When you are assembled in the name of our Lord Jesus and I am with you in spirit, and the power of the Lord Jesus is present, hand this man over to Satan, so that the sinful nature may be destroyed and his spirit saved on the day of the Lord" (1 Cor. 5:4–5). When faced with a situation where a Christian is enslaved to sin, and despite our best human efforts they refuse to repent, the church has additional supernatural resources available to it that individual Christians do not have.

Matthew 18 and 1 Corinthians 5 speak of church discipline, but the 1 Corinthians 5 passage speaks about power that is available to the church in "handing [a person] over to Satan." This is a drastic action, where the church has the authority to ask God to turn someone over to Satan so that they might experience enough pain that they will come to repentance. The authority, access, and promise of Christ's power are not given to *individuals* in this way. Because the church has the power to extend the discipline of God on an individual, it is the church — and not just the individual leaders — that is able to do more to help a sinning brother or sister.

The authority and power that God gives to the church makes all the difference in the world in some practical situations. For example, when those who are spiritually mature are trying to help couples who are struggling in their marriages, these couples often want to know the difference between what they can receive from the church and what they can receive from a Christian counselor outside the church. I believe there is a radical difference. A Christian counselor working outside the context of a local church can be helpful, but ultimately they are simply offering advice, which the marriage partners can take or leave as they see fit. But counseling that happens within the structure of the church, where a couple is connected relationally and accountable to others in the church body, carries with it a level of authority and power.

We often see couples in our church where one partner in the relationship simply refuses to do what they are being asked to do. In such situations the other spouse appears helpless. How will a wife with an extremely neglectful husband convince him to pay attention to her needs? How will a husband with a wife who is forming an unhealthy emotional attachment to another man convince her that this is dangerous? In these situations the church can come alongside the struggling couple with a certain level of authority and accountability. The church can ask two or three men to speak with a neglectful husband (or two or three women with the wandering wife) and encourage him to love his wife as Christ loves the church, offering both encouragement and accountability. If he refuses, the church can bring him under discipline and ask those who are members to separate themselves from him until he comes to recognize the seriousness of his neglect. The church can also ask God to do whatever is necessary to bring the person to repentance.

The unique power and authority that God gives to the church, combined with the diversity of spiritual gifts in the body of Christ and exercised under the care and guidance of leaders after God's own heart, enable us to accomplish more through the church than we could by ourselves or in any other group. Each of the three aspects we have looked at—spiritual gifts, leaders, and the church's unique access to God's power and authority—has been given to the church by God so that we might better accomplish our God-given mission.

HEARING FROM GOD

There is a great footnote to the story of Josh and Shelly and that little boy Charlie, who gave sacrificially to help this young family. Not only did Josh and Shelly get a wonderful house, but through a variety of circumstances God made sure that what Charlie had done for this family was made known to one of the pastors of Charlie's church. On the Sunday morning when the gifts for Josh and Shelly were collected, Charlie also gave his gift. After the collection, the pastor told Charlie that God had seen his act of faith and as a result, the church wanted to bless him for his willingness to give to others by providing him with a new hearing aid. Charlie was surprised and ecstatic. He had waited so long for a hearing aid, and this was an unexpected, wonderful gift! Through the church, Charlie experienced *both* the joy of seeing his own gifts multiplied *and* receiving the gifts of others. More was accomplished for Josh, Shelly, *and* Charlie through the church than could have ever been accomplished by people working alone.

CHAPTER 6

VISIBLE JESUS

One day early in Jesus' ministry, he met a young man from Bethsaida named Philip, and Jesus invited him to become his disciple (see John 1:43–51). Philip left everything he was doing and followed Christ. Now Philip was a sharp young man, well versed in his Hebrew (Old Testament) Scriptures, so it didn't take him long to suspect that his new teacher, Jesus, was truly the promised Messiah whom the Jews had been waiting for. Overjoyed at his discovery, Philip raced off to find his good friend Nathaniel and share his exciting news: "I've found the Messiah—and it's Jesus of Nazareth!" Disappointingly, Nathaniel didn't share Philip's excitement. After all, Nathaniel had never met Jesus and didn't know much about him except that he hailed from a small, backwater village in northern Israel. Nathaniel responded with a dismissive and cynical question—"Can anything good come out of Nazareth?"

But Philip was undeterred by Nathaniel's condescending response. Not wanting to argue with his friend, he simply told Nathaniel to come and see for himself. After sharing a few words with Jesus, Nathaniel, too, was convinced that Jesus was the Messiah, and Nathaniel moved from a place of cynical doubt to an open confession of faith. Nathaniel—like his friend Philip—joined the small, but growing group of disciples and became a follower of Jesus.

Later in the gospel of John (John 12:20–22), we meet Philip a second time. Several men from Greece have heard about Jesus, his teachings, and his miracles, and they want to meet with him.

115

Again, Philip serves as the connection point and leads these foreigners to Jesus, where he is out teaching the crowds. Once again, those who want to see Jesus are able to do so with the help of Philip. Thus, twice in John's gospel we find Philip bringing other people—both friends and foreigners—to Jesus, sharing the "good news" he has found.

Wouldn't it be great if we could all do evangelism that way, taking people to meet Jesus face-to-face? When our friends, family members, and neighbors have questions or express skepticism about Jesus, we could just bring them with their questions to Jesus. Wouldn't it be great to say to them, "I don't know the answer to that question ... let's go ask Jesus?" Obviously, we don't have the luxury Philip enjoyed. We don't have the same access to Jesus that Philip had—access to a tangible person.

Or do we?

STATE SENATOR ERNIE CHAMBERS VERSUS GOD

On September 14, 2007, in the district court of Douglas County Nebraska, on Docket 1075, page 462, Nebraska State Senator Ernie Chambers filed a petition for a permanent injunction against God. He wanted the court to order God to cease certain harmful activities, among them the making of terroristic threats. The petition accuses God of causing "fearsome floods, egregious earthquakes, horrendous hurricanes, terrifying tornadoes, pestilential plagues, ferocious famines, devastating droughts, genocidal wars, birth defects and the like."[50]

Over a year later, District Court Judge Marlon A. Polk formally dismissed the case because, as stated in legal terms, "service of process was not effectuated." Essentially, the case was dismissed because it was impossible for the court to find God in order to serve him with papers! In response, Senator Chambers argued that because God is omnipresent and omniscient, there was no need to serve him with papers, but the judge disagreed. He told the senator that if he really wanted to sue God, he would need to find a way of serving him with the papers.

Before you start wondering why a state senator would bother with such an unusual lawsuit, I should tell you that this was a tongue-in-cheek (but still very real) lawsuit that was intended to highlight the thousands of frivolous and unnecessary lawsuits the court system often has to deal with. Still, it effectively highlights the problem we've been talking about. Where do you go if you want to take people to meet with God?

We can't just bring non-Christians to someone they can touch and see, a person who can answer all of their questions face-to-face. We can't just sit down for coffee with Jesus and chat for a few hours. Obviously, the senator who brought the lawsuit did have a point, that as the Son of God, Jesus through his Spirit is present everywhere. But that's not what most people are asking for. Like Philip, we long to take our friends and neighbors to a real person with whom they can interact. Why don't we get the same opportunity that Philip had to take those we know to see Jesus?

JESUS MAKES VISIBLE THE INVISIBLE GOD

Interestingly, Philip provides us with a possible answer to this problem. In John 14, Philip faces a situation somewhat similar to our own. Philip also wants to see someone who is unseen and invisible. Thus, when Jesus declares to his disciples, "I am the way and the truth and the life. No one comes to the Father except through me" (John 14:6), Philip's ears perk up. He asks Jesus a reasonable question: "Lord, show us the Father, and that will be enough for us." Philip desperately wants to see God the Father, but as a good student of the Scriptures, Philip knows God is invisible. Yet Jesus has said that there is a way to "come to the Father" — to see the invisible God. Note how Jesus responds to Philip's question: "Don't you know me, Philip, even after I have been among you such a long time? Anyone who has seen me has seen the Father ... Don't you believe that I am in the Father, and that the Father is in me?" (14:9 – 10). Jesus is gently trying to teach Philip that *he* is the one who makes the invisible God visible.

In the beginning of his gospel, John, speaking of Jesus, says that "the Word became flesh and made his dwelling among us. We have seen his glory, the glory of the One and Only, who came from the Father, full of grace and truth" (John 1:14). John concludes his prologue with these words: "No one has ever seen God, but God the One and Only [i.e., Jesus], who is at the Father's side, has made him known" (1:18). In other words, Jesus came to make the invisible God visible. How? Two key words help us understand what John is saying here and why Jesus makes the invisible God visible to us: *full* (or *fullness*), and *grace*.

John tells us that Jesus "came from the Father, *full* of *grace* and truth"[51] (John 1:14), and "from the *fullness* of his *grace* we have all received one blessing after another" (1:16, italics added). In other words, Jesus was so full of grace that when people interacted with him, they were struck by something different. "He must have come from God," people would say — no other explanation was truly viable after meeting Jesus. Jesus, by his very nature, made the invisible God visible to sinful human beings. As Colossians 1:15 and 19 say: "He is the image of the invisible God ... For God was pleased to have all his *fullness* dwell in him."

Let me give you an example to explain this. In Denton, Texas, there is a well-known pastor named Tommy Nelson. As the senior pastor of Denton Bible Church, Tommy runs an extensive discipleship program. Every year he invites young men to come, live together, volunteer at the church, and study the Bible with him. They spend a great deal of time together. Because Tommy Nelson was trained for ministry at Dallas Theological Seminary, most of the young men mentored by Tommy end up making their way to Dallas Seminary. When these young men arrive on campus, they are immediately recognizable! A discerning eye can pick a "Tommy Nelson" student out of a crowd or a classroom. Why?

Because they have unique mannerisms, actions, attitudes, and ways of interpreting the Bible that look and feel a great deal like Tommy Nelson. Even though Tommy is not physically present on the Dallas Seminary campus, it is as if he really is there because of the presence of so many young men who make Tommy "visible" by their words, attitudes, and actions.

In some way I think that's what John is saying here about Jesus. Jesus was so "full" of God's grace that when you interacted with Jesus you knew, at some level, that you were dealing with the invisible God.

WHAT ABOUT US?

Perhaps you are thinking, *Well, that works great for Philip, but it doesn't solve our problem.* We're right back where we started! Philip couldn't see the invisible Father, but he could just take a good look at Jesus standing right in front of him. We don't have that option. Jesus came and went, and he is now ascended back to heaven and is seated at the right hand of the throne of God (Eph. 1:20–21), so that he is no longer physically present on the earth. For us, both God the Father *and* Jesus are invisible. What hope is there for those of us who, like Philip, want to show people Jesus or who want to see God? Fortunately, Ephesians 1 continues with verses 22–23: "God placed all things under his feet and appointed him to be head over everything for the church, which is his body, the *fullness* of him who fills everything in every way" (1:22–23, italics added).

Right now Christ is seated in heaven. But the Bible tells us that in some wonderfully mysterious way, Jesus is present here on earth through the church, which is his body. Just as our bodies are the ways in which our invisible thoughts are visibly communicated to this world, Jesus' body—the church—is the way in which he is made visible to this world. The church is God's way of making his *invisible* Son (to us on earth) *visible* again. Just as Philip was able to see the *invisible* Father by watching and observing Jesus, an unbelieving world can now look at the church and see the *invisible* Jesus made *visible*.

Karl Barth, one of the great theologians of the twentieth century, described the relationship between Jesus and the church this way:

> The community [church] is the earthly-historical form of existence of Jesus Christ himself. Jesus lives today as the Crucified and Risen One in a heavenly-historical form of existence ... but he does not live only and exclusively in this form, enclosed within it. He does not live above human history on earth, addressing himself to it only from above and from afar and from without. He himself lives in a special element of this history created and controlled by him. He therefore lives in an earthly-historical form of existence within it. This particular element of human history, this earthly-historical form of existence of Jesus Christ, is the Christian community.[52]

The church makes Jesus visible to the world in the same way Jesus made God the Father visible: by being *full of grace*. The church is called and empowered to make the ascended Christ visible in the world today by being absolutely and totally full of grace. In Ephesians 2:6–9 we read:

> God raised us up with Christ and seated us with him in the heavenly realms in Christ Jesus, in order that in the coming ages [*now and forever*] he might show the incomparable riches of his grace, expressed in his kindness to us in Christ Jesus. For it is by grace you have been saved, through faith—and this not from yourselves, it is the gift of God—not by works, so that no one can boast.

That is, God has poured out his grace on us in order that we might, in turn, be *demonstrations* of his grace to others. In other words, when people see God's grace in us, they will see Jesus in us, just like people saw God in the fullness of Jesus' grace.

There is, however, a fundamental difference between Jesus and his church in this respect, as Ephesians 2 makes clear. Jesus was full of grace in a unique way, as the incarnate Son of God. As God, he is the *source* of all grace and while present on the earth was uniquely able to communicate God visibly to the world. The church, by contrast, is full of grace, not because of some innate quality or natural characteristic, but because we are the *recipients* of the grace given through Jesus.

To summarize, Jesus makes the Father visible. And in turn, *the church makes Jesus visible.* Jesus is the fullness of God, and the church is where the fullness of Jesus is found. This striking parallel gives rise to Paul's stunning doxology in the middle of Ephesians: "Now to him who is able to do immeasurably more than all we ask or imagine, according to his power that is at work within us, to him be glory *in the church* and *in Christ Jesus* throughout all generations, for ever and ever" (Eph. 3:20–21, italics added). The glory of God is seen both in the person of the Son *and* in the collective witness of the church! As the body of Christ, recipients of God's grace, we visibly represent the work and person of Jesus to the world around us.

TWO PRODIGALS

In Luke 15 Jesus tells a story about a young man, around eighteen years old, who woke up one morning in a state of utter depression. Months earlier he had left his home, his family, and his father, a man well-loved and respected in the community. Wanting to make his own way in life, he was unable to see his father as anything more than a hindrance to his own selfish ambitions. One day, he went to his dad and demanded his share of the inheritance he would receive when his father died. Since his father was still alive, he was essentially telling his father that he wished he were dead. Oblivious to the public humiliation and private heartache he was inflicting on his father, the young man took his money and moved far from home.

At first, life was good, but over time he quickly burned through the money his father had accumulated through years and years of hard work. Suddenly, the young man found himself dirt poor, unpopular with his friends, and slaving away in the most degrading of jobs.

In the midst of his depression and facing a hopeless situation, the young man entertained a desperate thought—to return home, apologize to his dad, and beg for mercy. Back home, unknown to the young man, his father had been watching the road, day and night, for his son to return. On the day of his return, the father spotted him a long way off. Rising quickly from his seat, he began to run to his son. Townspeople gasped in horror to see a respectable man of means out running—undignified behavior for a wealthy landowner—but the father did not care. In joy, he welcomed his wayward son home, restoring him to his position in the family. He even threw a large party to commemorate his son's return.

Now the young man had a faithful and responsible older brother, who had been disgusted at his younger brother's disgraceful actions in leaving. With his brother's return, this older brother's disgust found a new target—their father. How could their father accept back this miserable wretch? And to throw him a party—the older brother just couldn't stomach it. He decided to teach his father a lesson about justice. Determined to publicly humiliate and privately crush his father, the older brother refused to attend the welcome-home party.

But again the grace of the father prevailed. Ignoring the culturally accepted behavior of the day, the father chose to leave the party to go in search of his older son. When his son lashed out in an angry, judgmental rage, the father responded in grace, offering love and forgiveness, just as he had with his younger son.

This story reveals to us the breadth and depth of the grace of God. The *breadth* of God's grace is seen because the father shows grace to both the younger son and the older son, both the immoral and the judgmental, both those who seek grace and those who do not know that they need grace. We see the *depth* of God's grace in the father's willingness to run to his younger son and to pursue his older son, in the complete and total forgiveness that the younger son experienced and that was offered to the older son, in God's continued acceptance of those whom he should have abandoned long ago. The church uniquely testifies to the reality of God's grace because the church is the recipient of the fullness of God's grace, both in its breadth and depth.

THE BREADTH AND DEPTH OF GOD'S GRACE IN THE CHURCH

Because the church is designed to be the most diverse institution possible (as we saw in chapter 2), it makes perfect sense that we would find the full *breadth* of God's grace expressed in the church. Consider the diverse types of people present in the church of Antioch in the first century. We do not know a great deal about the laypeople who belonged to that church, but we do know something about its leadership. There was Simeon of Niger, a black African prophet; Lucius of Cyrene, a Jew from the region of modern-day Libya; Manaen, the foster brother of King Herod Antipas and a member of elite social circles; Barnabas, a warm-hearted and spiritually wise apostle who came from a Jewish priestly family; and Paul, a former Pharisee who had been one of the primary persecutors of the early church. The diversity of the leadership of the church in Antioch should not surprise us given that it was the first church to incorporate both Jews and Gentiles. Because this church had so many diverse people from different backgrounds who had been saved by God's grace, the breadth of that grace was evident to all who visited the church.

The first-century church in Antioch was also a place where one could see the *depth* of God's grace. Paul tells us in 1 Timothy 1:16 that he felt he was the "worst of sinners," yet he was shown mercy so that God might display in him the depth of his grace.

Imagine walking into the church at Antioch and seeing the person who was once a blasphemer and chief persecutor of Christians worshiping Jesus! That was an overwhelming display of the depth of God's grace. How could God not only forgive such a man, but put him in leadership in the church? So evident was the breadth and depth of God's grace in this church that when Barnabas first arrived at Antioch, the most noticeable feature was "the evidence of the grace of God" (Acts 11:23).[53]

Barnabas was not the only one who noticed what was going on in the church at Antioch. According to Acts 11:26, the disciples were first called Christians at Antioch. "Christian" simply means "followers of Christ" or "part of the family of Christ." When the outside world in Antioch noticed the breadth and depth of God's grace visible in the church, they took to calling them "Christ-followers." The fullness of God's grace at the church in Antioch made Jesus Christ visible to those in the city, just as God intended.

The church's ability to manifest Jesus by being a recipient of the fullness of God's grace is not limited to the first century. Many churches today have used "cardboard testimonies" in their services. During a "cardboard testimony" service, people from the church come forward with a large piece of cardboard. On one side is a word or a short phrase describing their life before they experienced the transforming power of God's grace. It may read "gossip," or "alcoholic," or "lonely." The cardboard is then flipped over to show the result of how God's grace has transformed them — "speaker of love," "sober and free," or "friend of God"! Watching one of these cardboard testimony services is an overwhelmingly emotional experience. (If you have never seen one live, look one up on YouTube under "cardboard testimonies.")

As you watch testimony after testimony, it paints a picture of the breadth and depth of God's grace. You realize that so many different kinds of people — from drug addicts to abandoned children to nominal Christians — have been transformed by the grace of God. It also helps us to realize that God has graciously forgiven a whole variety of pretty awful stuff. You cannot watch such a display and have doubts about the mercy of God. Jesus and the saving grace of the gospel are clearly manifest through these powerful testimonies.

This is why Paul prays that the church in Ephesus might have "power, together with all the saints, to grasp how *wide and long and high and deep* is the love of Christ" (Ephesians 3:18, italics added). Grasping Christ's infinite love is a communal process. That's why it says "with all the saints." Because God's love for all his children is equal, when we share with one another the stories of God's love and grace, we all grow *together* to understand better the breadth and depth of God's love. And when people from different life situations and experiences together share with one another how they have been loved by God, the church is filled to the measure with "all the *fullness* of God" (Eph. 3:19)!

GRACE REMAINS FOR THE CHURCH

The fullness of God's grace can only be seen where the breadth and the depth of God's grace are evident. And the church is best positioned to showcase the extent of God's grace for one simple reason: no other group has needed as much grace as the church! I am at a loss to think of another group that has failed repeatedly as the church at living up to what God expects it to be. In the opening chapter of this book I presented Luther's assessment: *there is no greater sinner than the Christian church*. The failures of the Christian church are magnified by the glory and holiness of the God the church is called to represent to the world.

But if this is true—that the church is the greatest sinner—then the gospel teaches us that the converse is also true: there is no group who has received more grace than the Christian church (Rom. 5:20). Consider the local churches that Jesus confronts in Revelation 2–3. One is filled with idolatry; another with immorality; another with complacency; in another, love for God has grown cold; and another is spiritually dead. Jesus is stern with them, but he still graciously accepts them as his churches. What church in the New Testament wasn't rife with horrendous problems? The church in Corinth seems to be guilty of every possible sin, the churches in Galatia struggled with legalism, and the churches in Rome were judgmental and not good at accepting outsiders. And that is just the beginning.

Think about the Crusades, the Inquisition, the Peasant's Revolt, the Thirty-Years War, the Salem witch trials, Manifest Destiny, American slavery, European fascism, and modern sex-abuse scandals — to name just a few of the more egregious examples! Think of all the terrible things that the church universal as well as individual, local churches have committed, caused, condoned, refused to confront, or came late to the party on. It is unfathomably scandalous that God would continue to accept the church or use her to accomplish his purposes.

Yet he does.

God is not blind to the sins of the church. If you are like me, you have experienced firsthand the painful failures of the local church. If we are distressed when we hear a poorly crafted sermon, what must God think? If we feel angry when our hard-earned money, given in good faith to the church, is wasted, what must God feel? If we are mortified when a close friend at church betrays us and shares confidential information as a "prayer request," how must God respond? As disappointed as we are in the church, God has far higher expectations.

Yet God refuses to abandon the church. Is there any greater testimony to God's grace than this? In the story of the prodigal son, we see the beauty of the grace of the father reflected against the failures of his two sons. But who has failed more than the church? God's continued acceptance of his church, despite our repeated offenses and failures, is one of the ways in which we reveal the love of God to the world. Because so many people are ready to be done with church, God's infinite grace is highlighted because he continues to accept the church. The fact that

God still manifests his presence in the midst of a motley crew of legalistic, immoral, proud, lazy, hypocritical, and judgmental people proclaims his grace to this world in the loudest possible fashion. What other empire, organization, or group of humans has received as much grace as the church? No other group can point people to a gracious God like the church can.

GRACIOUS GOD, GRACIOUS CHURCH

At this point, though, we need to avoid a common misunderstanding of grace. Given the fact that our failures as a church highlight the scandalous grace of God, we may be tempted to think that the sins and mistakes of the church are actually a *good* thing, since they highlight God's grace. If God loves his church and accepts his people regardless of their behavior, why should the church ever grow in holiness? Won't God just continue to forgive, even as the church continues to fail? These are fair questions (cf. Rom. 6:1), but they reflect a misunderstanding of grace and God's true purpose for his church. Grace is given, not simply as a license to continue in sin, but in such a way that it leads to change and transformation, demonstrating the power of God. The church is shown scandalous grace so that it might become an *agent* of grace to others.

My dad became a Christian around the age of forty. Before that time he lived a religious life, but it was not the life of a genuine Christian. As he tells it, my father was trying to please God through external deeds while knowing deep inside that he had willfully disobeyed God's righteous standards. My father has never shared the specific details of his rebellious disobedience with me, but as I have gotten older, I have pieced together some idea of what his former life was like. Even though I don't know the specifics of his past, I do know that for the past forty years he has cried every time he sings the song "Amazing Grace."

Still, I know that my dad has received the grace of God in his life, not because he has told me or because of tears cried over a song, but because the grace of God has transformed him into an *agent* of grace to others. Saddened by Christians who took the grace of God for granted, my dad would tell me time and again, "Too many people stop reading after Ephesians 2:8–9, but you have to read verse 10." In this verse the apostle Paul writes, "For we are God's workmanship, created in Christ Jesus to do good works, which God prepared in advance for us to do." My father's point was simple: God has made us recipients of his grace for a reason. We receive grace in order to become agents of his grace to others, doing good works God has prepared for us to do.

How, exactly, is the church designed to be an agent of grace? While there are many ways we can exhibit and demonstrate God's grace to others, I would like to highlight three ways in particular: monetary collections, the practice of baptism, and the grace-gifts.

Collections

When we take an offering at church, it enables the church to become an agent of God's grace to others. In 2 Corinthians 8, Paul writes about the churches of Macedonia who have been recipients of God's grace and now earnestly desire to be agents of that same grace by giving of their financial resources. Paul writes that "they gave as much as they were able, and even beyond their ability. Entirely on their own, they urgently pleaded with us for the privilege of sharing in this service to the saints" (8:3–4). Paul calls their giving an "act of grace," and he urges the Corinthian church to excel in this "grace of giving" (8:6–7). Why? Because they themselves have received grace from God through Jesus Christ (8:9).

The idea to take an offering or a collection was not something invented by church leaders looking for creative ways to increase church revenue. From the earliest days of the Christian church, collecting money (to help those in need) has been an integral part of worship services. And this particular grace, the collection of funds for the poor, was a powerful witness to the watching world of the truthfulness of the gospel. Justin Martyr, who lived in the second century AD (born about AD 114), writes of the church, "And they, who are well to do and willing, give what each thinks fit." The money given was used to help widows and orphans, the sick, those in want, prisoners, travelers, "and in a word takes care of all who are in need."[54] This kind of giving was an effective way in which the early church proclaimed and demonstrated the grace of God to the world.

Tertullian, another leader in the early church, writes that many non-Christians were surprised by the degree of mutual care they observed in the church: "How they love one another!" Lucian, a non-Christian who wrote attacking the early Christian church, still conceded on one point: the members of the church were financially generous to one another. Julian, a fourth-century Roman emperor who was also antagonistic to Christianity, even wrote a letter to his Roman citizens encouraging them to *imitate* the charity of the Christian churches, commenting that they "support not only their poor, but ours as well."[55]

These witnesses to the grace of God, seen through the financial generosity of church members, are not limited to the early church. Thousands of examples abound today. For example, consider Project Turn Around, a ministry of Oak Cliff Bible Fellowship, a Dallas-area church. This ministry, supported with resources and volunteers from the church, reaches out to help students, schools, and urban communities. Over the twenty years of this successful ministry it has received national recognition, even from the secular media. Consistently, this ministry has pointed to the grace of God as the motivation and purpose behind the work that is done.

It is noteworthy that most parachurch organizations and other informal gatherings of Christians generally do not regularly take up a collection when they meet. I attended hundreds of chapel services at Dallas Seminary, and there was never a collection taken. When I worked at an inner city ministry, there was never a formal collection either. And when I would gather with a group of my friends at the local pub for theological discussions, we never passed a basket around to collect money. Interestingly, most parachurch organizations solicit money from those outside their ministry, but many systematically do not incorporate opportunities for those to whom they are ministering to particpate in the grace of giving. Now some might see this as a strength of those types of gatherings and wonder why the church needs to collect money at all. But as we have seen, the lack of a regular practice of giving is actually a sign that the fullness of God's grace is not being manifested by these gatherings. As we have seen, biblically and historically, the practice of taking an offering for the needy is an important way God enables the church to be an agent of grace.

Baptism

In my office I have a framed note from a woman in our congregation. The penmanship is poor, but the note is one of my most treasured possessions. The first time that I, as a senior pastor, invited people to respond to the call of Christ for salvation, this woman came forward after the service. She was in a wheelchair, and she had difficulty speaking as a result of some physical limitations. I spoke with her about Jesus' love, and she indicated that she was ready to surrender complete control of her life to him. Afterwards, I learned some additional details about this woman. She had been part of a Bible study, meeting with others at a group home, but she had resisted giving her life to Jesus. After some time, though, the Holy Spirit overcame her resistance, and she reluctantly came to a service. Our meeting that Sunday morning was only the second time she had attended church, but it changed her life forever.

As time went by, this woman — now a new believer in Christ — continued to participate in her weekly Bible study, but would now joyfully share with others that she was a Christian. Eventually, she asked to be baptized. Special arrangements were made, and someone met with her to ask if she would publicly share her story with the church. Although it would be a struggle for her to communicate, she insisted on sharing her own story and repeatedly turned down our misguided suggestion that someone else read it for her. In her testimony, she shared her full story with the church. We learned that she had not, in fact, been born with her physical disability, but had suffered a horrific, debilitating accident several years ago. Her husband had left her and had taken the children with him as well, claiming she was now incompetent as a mother and unable to properly care for them. She ended up living in a group home and had been filled with a consuming hatred for God. She had been convinced that he was the cause for all of the problems in her life, that he should have stopped this from happening to her.

For years, this woman had nurtured her anger and resentment, but, as she shared that morning, God had continued to pursue her with his patient, unrelenting love, and his grace had finally saved her from her hatred and sin. She spoke about her ongoing suffering and the daily battle against her pain, but also spoke of her new hope in Christ. She was now ready to live for him. As she finished her testimony, the room was quiet except for the sound of people sobbing and weeping. There was a real sense that God's Spirit was present in the room that morning.

Baptism is one of the most beautiful gifts God gives to his church. Through baptism, the church trumpets the grace of God so that everyone can hear. In Ephesians 4, after Paul writes that we are the recipients of God's grace, he begins to encourage the church to be an agent of grace. He writes: "There is one body and one Spirit — just as you were called to one hope when you were called — one Lord, one faith, one baptism; one God and Father of all" (4:4–6). This list shows us the source and the means of God's grace. The Spirit, the Lord, and God the Father are the source of grace, and the body (the church) is the recipient of God's grace. Faith and hope are the channels by which we receive the amazing gift of God's grace. And that leaves us with baptism, which, at first glance, seems a bit out of place. But, baptism is the *ceremony* of grace.

During the celebratory event of baptism, we publicly confess that we are *recipients* of grace and publicly commit ourselves to be *agents* of grace. Whenever we publicly baptize an individual, God is displaying his grace in and through the church, and we are reminded that God wants our lives to show his grace to others.

The woman whom I baptized that morning did just that. She took her experience of the grace of God and began sharing it with everyone in her group home. Many of the people in her group home have also come to understand and receive the love of God through her story. Her experience of God's gracious love has turned her into an agent of that same grace as she shares it with others. One of my great joys every Sunday is to see this woman and a growing number of her friends attending church.

Baptism is the sign and the celebration of God's grace and a reminder of our ongoing call to be agents of that grace to others.

Grace-Gifts

Ephesians 4:7 says, "To each one of us grace has been given as Christ apportioned it" (cf. Rom. 12:6). First Peter 4:10 expands on this idea even further: "Each one should use whatever gift he has received to serve others, faithfully administering God's grace in its various forms." In a previous chapter, we discussed the idea of spiritual gifts, unique gifts given by God to manifest his presence in our lives as we minister his grace to others. Interestingly enough, these gifts are also known as "grace-gifts." The Greek word used to refer to these spiritual gifts (*charismata*) is related to the Greek word for grace (*charis*). These God-given grace-gifts are what enable us to share God's grace with others. It becomes a reciprocal process as we receive grace, share it with others, and are in turn blessed to receive the ministry of others in our lives as well.

To grasp the way God intends these gifts to function, consider the example of a farmer waking up on a typical weekday morning. The farmer eats his breakfast and gets enough energy from his breakfast to carry him through the work for that morning. While he is working, that same farmer will also be doing his part to provide food for others, all while using the energy he has received from the breakfast provided for him earlier that day. In this sense, the farmer both benefits *from* the work of others as well as brings a benefit to others *through* his work. In a similar way, we receive grace *from* God when others serve us using the gifts God has given them. At the same time, we are also enabled to minister to others *through* the work we do with our grace-gifts. The ministry of others—whether through a teaching, a word of encouragement, or an act of service—strengthens us and enables us to serve others in turn. The gifts become channels for the giving and receiving of God's grace.

This is why Paul begins his aside in Ephesians 3:2–13 by saying, "Surely you have heard about the administration of God's grace that was given to me *for you*" and then ends by saying "[do not] be discouraged because of my sufferings *for you*, which are your glory" (italics added). Paul *received* grace from God in his calling as an apostle and through the ministry God assigned to him for the Ephesians and others (Eph. 4:7–13; cf. 1 Cor. 15:9–10). And when Paul exercised his grace-gifts, the church *received* grace through his teaching and equipping of the saints in Ephesus. Whenever a pastor preaches, or someone shares a word of encouragement or brings a meal to a person who is sick, grace is given.

As a result of this reciprocal process of giving and receiving grace, the church reaches "unity in the faith and in the knowledge of the Son of God and becomes mature, attaining to the whole measure of the *fullness* of Christ" (Eph. 4:13, italics added). When everyone in the church exercises their gifts of grace, the church is filled with grace and Jesus is visible to all.

LYING ABOUT GOD

What if our church is not an agent of grace? What if we have more often than not experienced the opposite of grace in church? This is a real problem because while the church is a place of grace, *it also has to be a place of ungrace.* Church must be a place where all of us—chronic complainers, self-serving manipulators, and judgmental hypocrites included—are welcome and accepted. As a result, church is a place where we are guaranteed to experience negativity, manipulation, and hypocrisy. But because God is so gracious, he patiently works with us, teaching us and transforming us into agents of his grace as we learn to daily receive his grace. While we may long for the church to be a place where every person is well-behaved, every service is excellent and edifying, and every experience is life changing and powerful, the church—if it is to be the church of grace that God intends—will always need to be a place for messed-up, hypocritical, and judgmental people. That's what the world needs.

We are not *naturally* gracious people. Our natural tendency is to see the immorality, hypocrisy, and incompetence of the church and walk away. But when we walk away from the church because it is not what we want it to be or even all that it can be, we end up proclaiming to the world a false god—a legalistic, judgmental god. By embracing the church as a fallen mess of sinful people, filled with faults and failures, we proclaim the true God—one who is full of all grace—to the whole world. Mike Foster, in his contribution to the book *unChristian*, says it this way:

> Why should we stay and work on these problems? Why not just blow the whole thing up? Because, first off, no one likes a quitter, and second, lobbing hand grenades on the bride of Christ takes zero talent or effort. I also think this really ticks God off. My five-year-old child complains and whines when things are not the way she wants them, but courageous men and women roll up their sleeves and get busy. I want to

be an active participant in putting back together the broken pieces.[56]

So we stay and serve, not because the church is perfect — far from it. We stay and we serve because it is the very grace we show to others in the church that makes the church the place of grace that God designed it to be.

WOULD PHILIP BRING PEOPLE TO CHURCH TODAY?

Let me close with a final clarification. When I speak about the church as a "place" of grace and a "means" of grace, I might have given you the impression that a non-Christian needs to come to a church service if they want to meet Jesus. Certainly, non-Christians do see Jesus in a healthy church (1 Cor. 14:24–25). But what I really mean to say is not just that people see Jesus in actual church gatherings — they see Jesus *through* the church. This can happen when the local body of believers is gathered together to worship, or it can be as individual participants in the church take the grace they have received from God into their workplaces, coffeehouses, book clubs, and neighborhoods.

The other day at the post office I noticed people coming in to get their mail. I tried to imagine what it would be like if everyone got their mail this way — it would be a logistical nightmare and highly impractical! Instead, to run more efficiently, the post office sends mail carriers out into neighborhoods and businesses all over the country. Postal workers gather together at the post office to receive mail, process it for delivery, and then distribute it to those to whom the mail is addressed.

I believe that this is what God intends for his church to be like. God wants to deliver the grace of Jesus to people from every tribe, in every nation, and among every people group on the planet. While it is possible for those who are looking for God's grace to come to the church to receive it, it is much more natural and effective to have that grace delivered to them, right where they are, where they work and live. In order for the grace of Jesus to be delivered effectively, the agents of his grace must first gather together as the church to receive his grace before they can deliver it to the people to whom God wants them to deliver it.

So let's go back to where we started: Where would you take someone if you wanted them to meet Jesus today? If our friend Philip were alive today, he just might take them to the gathered assembly of Christ-followers — the church — where Jesus can be seen as people receive and celebrate the grace of God. Or, he might take Jesus to them through acts of grace made possible because he himself had seen Jesus and received grace through his participation in the church.

VISIBLE JESUS

The world still needs to see Jesus. The world still needs to interact with him in a tangible way, and the church is the means by which God enables that to happen. As the fullness of Jesus on earth, the church manifests the invisible Jesus, making him visible through word and deed. The church is able to do this because it is the primary recipient of the fullness of God's grace. When redeemed sinners of all shapes and sizes gather together as Christ's church, the breadth and depth of God's grace become visible for all to see. By receiving God's grace, the church is empowered to be agents of grace. Yet, ironically, even when the church fails to be the agent of grace God calls it to be, it still manifests a gracious God to the world as God continues to lovingly accept his church, despite its failures.

CONCLUSIONS

"My life after church has become a life after church. What I thought I was walking away from now haunts my dreams and stirs my longing heart. God's vision for his church is so magnificent, so beautiful, that we can never leave it without leaving him." So concludes Brian Sanders in his provocative book *Life after Church.*[57]

The church is God's church, and it is a result of his vision. We can and should take issue with the varying ways in which God's vision for church has been manipulated, perverted, and corrupted. We can and should acknowledge that the church is the chief sinner. We can and should recount the way that the church has failed us and we have failed the church. But in the end, God's vision for the church remains. The church is a creative act of God. God the Father designed and decreed the first creation, and he has designed and decreed the creation of the church. God the Son spoke the first creation into existence, and he has spoken the church into existence. And just as the Holy Spirit hovered over the deep in the first creation, the Spirit of God was given at Pentecost to remain with the church as the constant, abiding presence of God. The church is a unique creation of God.

Despite the apparent flaws that sin introduced into the world we live in, it is still a place of great beauty. The same is true of the church. Despite the presence of sin and the ongoing, persistent failures of the church, it remains a community of great beauty. Perhaps a painful experience in your past has obscured the beauty of God's church for you. Perhaps you feel like the narrator in the *Shepherd of Hermas*, who, when he first meets the church, sees her as an aged and unattractive old woman. Yet, as he learns to confess his own sin and grows in his understanding of grace, she becomes younger and more beautiful each time he sees her.[58]

Let me encourage you to take a second look at God's bride and discover the hidden beauty of his design for his people. What other gathering of people can compare to the picture God paints for us in his church, a community that experiences his divine presence, achieves unity in diversity, provides true community, grows to be like his Son, and accomplishes more together, and makes Jesus visible for all the world to see? The church is truly a gift from God, given for our benefit and his glory.

WHY CHURCH?

In his autobiography, Johnny Cash shares his own thoughts on our tendency to focus on the failures, shortcomings, and problems in the church rather than appreciating her for her inherent beauty, as God designed her:

> If we are going to start nit-picking on what's right or what's wrong with this or that church, we could soon forget what we need a church home for in the first place ... I need a spiritual foundation here on the earth that we have to walk around on. I need a spiritual anchor that I can reach back and grab hold of when I begin to drift. I'm human, and I need all the help I can get. I never thought church membership would be important to me ... Of course it isn't as important as believing, and you can worship God anywhere, but I need everything that He has to offer to give me support and courage.[59]

This same truth is illustrated beautifully in an old story that a friend recently shared with me. A man who had once been an integral part of a church body had slowly cut back on his involvement at church to the point where he was no longer attending. The pastor of the church decided to pay him a visit.

It was a cold winter's evening. When the pastor arrived at the man's home, he was cordially greeted, and the two men sat down for a conversation in front of a warm fire. The man waited for the pastor to begin speaking, while they both stared at the fire. After a minute or two of awkward silence, the pastor took the fire tongs, carefully picked up a brightly burning ember and placed it all alone, away from the flames on the hearth. Then he sat back in his seat. The two men watched together as slowly the once red-hot ember began to fade until it was cold and dead.

The pastor then stood up, picked up the cold, dead ember and placed it back into the middle of the fire. Immediately the ember was ablaze again with the light and heat of the burning wood around it.

A smile of understanding crept across the man's face. He led the pastor to the door and said with a tear in his eye, "Thank you for coming. I will be back next Sunday."

A MESSAGE FOR YOU

For Those Currently Involved in a Local Church

Let me begin by saying "thank you" to you for putting up with the failures and mistakes of the church. It can be exasperating sometimes, I know. Even as I write these words, I am personally involved in some difficult and challenging situations in our church. Even though I am a pastor and a leader in God's church, I know all too well the temptation to pack up your bags and leave town. I know what it feels like to want to quit the church. In my head and heart, I've done it many times. But I thank God for those of you who have chosen to stick it out. You have not given up on the church, even though you have endured difficult people and painful situations.

I am also confident, however, that you have experienced some amazing and wonderful things through the church. Let me encourage you to use this book and the material you have just read to consider how it compares to the local church you currently attend, not with an eye toward criticism and judgment, but as an honest, constructive assessment of your own faith community.

We all need to pause periodically and evaluate how well our experience of church matches with God's vision. Is your church as diverse as it could be? Is it actively seeking to do the whole mission of God? Does it put enough importance on proclaiming God's Word and celebrating the Lord's Supper? Does it offer true Christian hospitality? Does it have godly leaders?

Furthermore, take these principles and discuss them with Christians who may not be currently involved in a local church. Remind them that the church needs them ... and they need the church.

For Those Attending Church but Not Truly Engaged

Throughout this book I have argued that the church is designed for our benefit. But in truth, the church will not be of much benefit to us if we are not actively engaged and participating in it. If we simply view ourselves as people who "go to church" — never recognizing that we "are the church" — more than likely we will fail to reap the benefits of God's design.

This past spring I took my children to the San Diego Wildlife Park. There we saw a wide variety of animals. Like going to the zoo, it was possible to observe the animals, to study them, and even to enjoy looking at them. But we always remained separated from them, at a distance. Beyond looking at them and reading the signs, we received no substantial benefit from our interaction with them, nor did they receive much from us.

Compare the experience of visiting the zoo or a wildlife park with that of owning a pet. When you own a pet, you can share your love with the animal and can receive affection back from it. Taking care of a pet requires a certain amount of self-sacrifice, and you can experience, firsthand, devotion and dependence. Obviously, there is a big difference between owning a pet and going to the zoo. In the same way there is a difference between *being* the church and *going to* church. Simply showing up to a church building week after week to watch and observing the activities is a bit like going to the zoo (sometimes this seems to be literally true!). There is plenty to see and some interesting things to learn, but the benefits are limited since we remain at a distance from others; we aren't really engaged in a meaningful way. When we become part of the church, however, our level of involvement rises; and as our involvement rises, we experience more and more the benefits we have talked about in this book.

For Those Considering Switching Churches

Is it ever appropriate to switch to another church? Absolutely. There are, however, two dangers to avoid when you are evaluating your participation in a particular church. The first is to develop a habit of hopping from church to church, refusing to settle down, always searching for that "perfect" church. I have found that people who are always looking and searching may have some attraction to the church, but they do not truly *love* the church. Love requires a willingness to accept the church as she is, flaws and all. Those who have made a habit out of church-hopping should heed the words of Dietrich Bonhoeffer:

> If we do not give thanks daily for the Christian fellowship in which we have been placed, even where there is no great experience, no discoverable riches, but much weakness, small faith and difficulty; if on the contrary, we only keep complaining to God that everything is so paltry and petty, so far from what we expected, then we hinder God from letting our fellowship grow according to the measure and riches which are there for us all in Jesus Christ.[60]

The second danger to avoid is that of staying where God is no longer calling you to be. There are a whole host of reasons God may call someone away from one church to another. The church in which you are engaged may be unwilling to reform itself and may continue to resist gracious attempts at helping it become what God wants it to be. Or the church may, in fact, be a false church, where the gospel is not proclaimed. It may be a church where the leaders are not committed to the full mission of Jesus or the sacraments are not properly done. The church may be abusive or neglectful of the people under its care.

I confess that I would not be where I am today if my parents hadn't had the courage to leave the church where they had first become Christians because certain leaders in the church refused to accept me in grace. In addition, you may be at a healthy, God-honoring church, and God may be summoning you to shift from one church to begin serving and engaging in ministry at another church. A longtime member of our church, who had spent many years on our pastoral staff, came to me one day after retiring and told me that God was calling him and his wife to take their gifts and go and help a smaller church nearer to their home. Though sad at their leaving, we were glad for their responsiveness to God's call to serve. All things considered, there may be several reasons why God is calling you to shift from one church to another. But if you are hopping from church to church, without any end in sight, it's time to stop.

For Those Not Involved in a Local Church

My encouragement to you is to reconsider what you may be missing. I am truly sorry for the ways in which you have been hurt or disappointed by the church. I am sorry for the manifold failures of the church. But can we not agree that the design of the church is itself a beautiful thing? The vision God has laid out for the church is not easy, I admit. To experience God in worship, to bring unity out of diversity, to find and experience true community, to grow and help others grow to spiritual maturity, to accomplish more in this world, and to make Jesus visible in this world are infinitely difficult, but they are worth devoting ourselves to. Through the power of God's Spirit, the church can and often is what God intends it to be. Through the ministry of God's church, we catch glimpses of future glory.

Let's be honest. You can invest your time in many different things. But are these things, the groups and activities that fill your days, worthy of the God who made you? And are you experiencing the full breadth and depth of God's grace, available through his church? Are you a senior adult involved in a group that only fellowships with other senior adults? Or a young adult who never interacts with people outside your small group of other young adults? Don't settle for a Christian social club. Settling for groups that make you comfortable or are filled with people just like you is easy but ultimately fruitless. Don't limit your children to the experience of God they have in your family. Don't rob yourself of God's gift of church by trying to live out your faith on your own. Embrace God's beautiful design for the church.

For All of Us

Finally, we should all be reminded that Jesus himself was consumed with zeal for God's house (John 2:17). Jesus was not apathetic, negligent, or complacent about the church of his day. And when he ascended to heaven, that same zeal continued to inform his love for his church, even to the point of discipline (see Rev. 2–3). Being fully engaged in the life of the church, furious about her shortcomings, and graciously working for her survival … well, that's what it means to be like Christ. That's what it means to be *zealous* for the church—to love her as Christ does.

In the final verses of the final chapter of the final book of the Bible, we have these two statements from the lips of Jesus: "I … have sent my angel to give you this testimony for the churches" (Rev. 22:16), and "Yes, I am coming soon" (22:20). The first statement reminds us that Jesus' testimony is for the churches. Not for individuals. Not for some ethereal universal church. But for genuine local churches—both those seven historical churches listed in the early chapters of Revelation and Christ's local churches today.

The second statement tells us that Jesus is coming soon, and combined with the first statement it means that he expects that when he returns, his people will be engaged and actively involved in local churches all over the world. The form of the church — whether a house church, a megachurch, a denominational church, an underground church, a microchurch, or a simple church — is not what matters, as long as it is a *true* church.

But how does Jesus know that the local church won't become irrelevant? How does he know that the local church won't be overwhelmed by its own sin and failures? How does he know that the local church won't be cast aside in favor of some better grouping of Christians? It is because Jesus is the Lord of the church — it's his creation! And he has promised that not even hell itself can overcome the church (Matt. 16:18). Despite the grand failures of the church over the centuries, the church represents God's future plans for his people, and his design is infinitely better than anything we can come up with in our own wisdom.

Let's not forget that Jesus knows our needs better than we know ourselves. You and I have become experts at determining what we *want*. We know, without a doubt, that we *want* a community of people who look like us, where we can be comfortable. We *want* a place where we see immediate, visible results, a group that the world thinks is cool and inoffensive, and a community where everyone follows our rules and agrees with our understanding of God. We *want* a place where we can avoid the ugliness of sin, a place where we are in charge and always get our way, a community that demands little of our precious time, money, and energy.

But what we really *need* is a place where we can gather together and experience God's unique presence, even though there may be times when we don't always feel it or see it. We *need* a place where we can be changed and transformed into the likeness of Christ, even if it is a painfully slow process. We *need* a community that reveals the wonderful diversity of God's creation, even if we have to strive for unity in the midst of our differences. We *need* a place where we can experience true community, even at the risk of betrayal and suffering. We *need* a team of people committed to the whole mission of God, striving and accomplishing more together, even if it means we sometimes experience dysfunctional team dynamics. And we *need* a community where the greatness of our sin and failure only serves to magnify the wonder of God's mercy and his grace, where God's work in salvation is powerfully evident to the world, and where Christ is made visible to all.

We *need* the church. And that's why the church is such a precious gift from God. It is a gift that meets our greatest needs and brings glory to God. It's a gift that shows us what we were really created for. And it's a gift for which I am profoundly grateful.

APPENDIX

This appendix deals with some important clarifications for the interested reader. In this section I cover five important questions:

1. What is church?
2. What is the relationship between the *local* church and the *universal* church?
3. Is God the center of weak churches?
4. What is my bias toward the church?
5. What should we do with the institutional nature of the church?

WHAT IS THE CHURCH?[61]

Twenty-five people gather together every Wednesday night at a young couple's house. There is no recognizable organizational structure, no set pattern that the meeting follows. *Is this a church?* Ten thousand people gather together on Sunday morning in a purposefully built structure. The gathering is run by ordained clergy and follows a set liturgy. *Is this a church?* One hundred students are enrolled in a theology class that meets twice weekly. *Is this a church?* Eight women get together every Tuesday morning for Bible study and prayer. *Is this a church?* Fifty thousand men gather in a football stadium one Saturday and sing praises to God. *Is this a church?* Three Christians work together at a large corporation in the same department. They meet before work for a few minutes of prayer every day. *Is this a church?*

There are endless varieties of ways in which Christians can gather together. How do we determine which of these gatherings constitute a "church" and which do not? This is more than a mere academic question. The benefits I have presented in this book are benefits particularly given to the church, not to other groups that meet, even if the people gathering are Christians. Biblical passages that speak of the church are immediately relevant only to groups that are, in fact, churches. So what constitutes a church?

Theologians commonly agree on the broad answer to this question. Wherever the Spirit of Christ is present in *church-forming* activity, there is the church. The Holy Spirit is present all around us in many different roles, but when he is present in a group in his role as *church-creator*, then that group is a church. In other words, if the *Spirit* has identified a group of people as a church and is intentionally enabling them to be a church, that group is a church. It may be a bad church or a weak church, but in the eyes of God, it's a church. To put it simply, God determines what constitutes a church, since he is the creator of the church.

But how can we know, specifically, if the Spirit of Christ is present in a group of people, making them into a church? There are always groups of people who call themselves Christians but who clearly do not follow the teachings of Christ. Similarly, there may be groups that call themselves a church but are not necessarily a church (and vice versa).

It may be helpful to start by considering how we determine if a person is a Christian. We know that a person is a Christian if the Spirit identifies them as a Christian—if they are *born again* by the work of God's Spirit. In addition, there are *visible signs* that attest to the Spirit's presence in their lives (1 Cor. 12:3; Gal. 5:22–23). Likewise, a group is a church if the Spirit identifies them as a church and there are *visible signs* of his presence among them.

Identifying specific features of the Spirit's presence is not universally agreed upon, but there do seem to be certain characteristics that are universally present in a Spirit-created church. First and foremost, there must be at least two or three people gathered together in Jesus' name (Matt. 18:20). A church is a gathering of people in a specific place who have gathered for the purpose of calling on the name of the Lord Jesus Christ (1 Cor. 1:2). The Greek word for church (*ekklesia*) means "assembly," and the Old Testament background to the word demands that this gathering is not just any assembly, but a regular assembling of God's people around God's presence. If Joe Christian and Jane Christian never actually meet together, they are both Christians, but they do not constitute a church. If they are not getting together to call upon the name of Jesus and simply happen to meet together for a local school board meeting, the local school board meeting is not a church. Furthermore, to gather in Jesus' name and to call on his name is to confess that Jesus is Lord, which is indisputable evidence of the Spirit's presence (1 Cor. 12:3). If a group of seekers gathers together who have not yet acknowledged the lordship of Christ, this group is not a church (this does not mean that everyone present must be believers).

Furthermore, there are some additional factors that should be evident if two or three people have gathered in Jesus' name and the Spirit is present, which then makes them a church:

(1) *A church is committed to the whole mission of God.* To gather in Jesus' name is to be committed to what Jesus was committed to: seeing God's will done on earth as it is in heaven. Coworkers who gather together for prayer every morning are doing something wonderful, but they are not a church because the church is called to do more than just pray. The church must also preach, teach, disciple, show mercy, give to those in need, and so on. There is no sphere of existence that Christ does not claim lordship over through the church (Eph. 1:22–23).

(2) *A church is committed to the preaching of Word and the right exercise of the sacraments.* Church is where Jesus is uniquely present in the midst of his people. The Holy Spirit manifests Jesus' presence especially through the proclamation of the Word and through the sacraments of baptism and communion. Therefore,

an accountability group that meets together to discuss life but never hears the Word preached or celebrates the Lord's Supper or baptism is not a church.

(3) *A church confesses its sins and exercises church discipline.* When the Holy Spirit is present in a group, he causes people to say, "Forgive us our sins." To assemble in Jesus' name is to stand in God's presence on the basis of Jesus' righteousness alone. Correspondingly, to assemble in Jesus' name requires removing those Christians who unrepentantly and unashamedly defy Christ's commands in blatant, habitual, and contaminating ways (1 Cor. 5).

(4) *A church bases membership on Christ alone.* The Spirit has created the church to be a group where people of differing races, socioeconomic backgrounds, genders, ages, experiences, and spiritual giftednesss come together (1 Cor. 12:12–13). Christian medical groups are not churches because in order to participate in such groups, it is necessary to be a health care professional as well as a Christian.

(5) *A church covenants together.* In Matthew 18, the central passage mentioned above, the two or three Christians have agreed to gather together intentionally and regularly for the purpose of being the church. Church is a group with some level of commitment to meet and share life together. If a group of men come together one time for a Christian rally, the gathering may provide encouragement, but it is not a church.

(6) *A church desires unity.* The church-forming Spirit is also the Spirit of unity. Therefore a church is a group that strives for unity internally and with other churches. To strive for unity with other churches is at least to be aware of and open to other churches as well as to be committed to the practices and patterns common to churches. For as many differences as there are between churches, there is a remarkable amount of commonality in practices. For example, churches have always taken up collections for the needy, and to be a church is to recognize the need to be united with others in this action.

(7) *A church is led by pastoral leaders.* When the Spirit is present in church-forming activity, he raises up leaders to shepherd the group. Spirit-gifted and ordained leaders of the church function differently than leaders in the world (Matt. 20:25). Their activity is best described using terms like pastor, bishop, priest, elder, deacon, teacher, minister, and servant. Their leadership is characterized by love, sacrifice, and servanthood.

(8) *A church is grace-based.* To gather in the name of Christ is to exist in the grace of Christ. Participation in church is voluntary. There are no entrance fees or grades earned for performance. Merit-based institutions such as Christian schools are not churches because they are not fundamentally grace-based.

In considering these factors, we must note that Jesus never considers his twelve disciples to be a church during his earthly ministry. Their presence as a group pointed to the coming church, but they were not themselves a church. The Spirit had not yet been given and therefore could not be present in church-forming activity. Moreover, women and Gentiles were not included among the Twelve. That's why even after the twelve had been called, Jesus spoke of the building of the church as something still future (see Matt. 16:16 – 19). The coming of the Spirit at Pentecost was the beginning of the church.

These are some of the most important evidences of the presence of the Spirit in church-forming activity. It is important to also note what is *not* determinative of the Spirit's presence: size, church structure, denominational affiliation, type of building (or lack thereof), order of service, style of music, length of meeting together, times of meeting, having paid or unpaid staff, using the phrase "church" to identify themselves, length of incorporation, or official governmental recognition.

So are the twenty-five people who get together every Wednesday evening at the young couple's house a church? It depends. Is the Word of God preached? Is there unity? Are they committed to the whole mission of God? Do they take communion together?

Is the gathering of ten thousand people on Sunday morning a church? It depends. Do they exercise church discipline? Do they have pastoral leaders? Are they diverse in ethnicity, socioeconomic background, experience, giftedness, gender, and age? Are they aware of and open to other churches?

Are the one hundred students enrolled in the theology class, the eight women in Bible study, the fifty thousand men in the football stadium, and the three coworkers churches? Probably not. They may be useful for advancing the kingdom of God, but they are not what I am referring to in this book as church.

The above eight criteria help to delineate what I believe the Bible means by the word *church* and to differentiate "church" from groups like women's Bible studies, Christian colleges, Christian families, Christian business persons' associations, worship conferences, and Christian aid organizations. All Christian groups exist somewhere on a continuum that ranges from groups that exhibit all these characteristics on one end, to groups that have none of these characteristics on the other. To the extent that a group is closer to the ideal of a church spelled out here, the more the benefits discussed in this book are applicable.

UNIVERSAL CHURCH OR LOCAL CHURCH?

When I use the word *church*, do I mean Church with a capital "C" or church with a lowercase "c"? In other words, are we talking about the invisible, universal "Church" made up of all who are believers in Jesus, or the local "church," those tangible, visible assemblies of believers meeting together in everything from parks to cathedrals? In this book I am referring, for the most part, to the latter.

The exact relationship between the local church and the universal church is complicated. Most references in the New Testament are to the local church, but some important ones refer primarily to the universal church. (There are also a few passages in which it is not clear which referent is in the writer's mind.) For our purposes it is sufficient to say that the universal church and the local church are intimately connected. The easiest way to think about it is: if you want to find the universal church, go to your local church. That is why most statements in the New Testament that speak of the universal church also have reference to the local church.

For example, when Christ says, "I will build my church" (Matt. 16:18), he is talking about the universal church, but he is also talking about the local church. Christ is not building his universal church *apart* from local churches but *through* them. Consider a simple analogy. When God says "Let us make man in our image" (Gen. 1:26), he is referring *both* to the creation of humankind *and* to the creation of a specific man and woman. In a similar way, references to the universal church *include* the local church. You cannot be for the universal church but against the local church; it would be like being for humanity but against humans! It just doesn't make sense.

GOD CAN'T BE THE DESIGNER AND CREATOR OF THE CHURCHES I HAVE ATTENDED!

One of the key verses for the special needs ministry at our church is Psalm 139:14: "I praise you because I am fearfully and wonderfully made." Why would a special needs ministry focus on that verse? Because it is easy for those with physical or mental disabilities to forget that they are still God's creation. Adam and Eve were not autistic. But that does not mean that someone who is born with autism is less a creation of God or bears less of the image of God. In Psalm 139:13 David speaks for all of us when he says to God, "You created my inmost being; you knit me together in my mother's womb." Every single person is a creation of God in spite of our shortcomings and disabilities.

Sometimes we read the first few chapters of Acts as we read the first few chapters of Genesis. The first church was seemingly perfect just as Adam and Eve were. We then look at churches today and see failure, and we think that this somehow means that these churches are not designed and created by God. But the truth of the matter is that God is the designer and creator of all true churches. Our flaws and failures as humans do not nullify the fact that we are created by God and still bear his image. The flaws and failures of churches do not nullify the fact that God is the designer and creator of our churches today.

OF COURSE YOU ARE FOR CHURCH; YOU ARE A PASTOR!

There is an alleged story of a man who saw the atheistic philosopher David Hume up early one morning, heading to hear noted evangelist George Whitfield. The man was shocked to see Hume and said to him, "I thought you didn't believe all this stuff about God."

Hume replied, "I don't, but *he* does."[62]

There is no better person to listen to about the church than someone who believes passionately in it. I want to be up front that I am passionately committed to what the local church can and should be. I do not believe in church because I am a pastor; I am a pastor because I believe in church.

HASN'T THE CHURCH BECOME JUST ANOTHER INSTITUTION?

"The problem with the local church is that it is an institution." On one hand, this is a fair indictment if it means that the church is often *overly institutional*. The essence of church is not hierarchies, policies, committees, buildings, rules, programs, and budgets. The essence of church is relationships with God and others. Whenever programs and policies become the dominant focus of church, something has gone terribly wrong.

However, it is impossible for the church not to be an institution because the church that Jesus is building is not some ethereal, disembodied ideal—it is a real community, filled with real people. In this respect the church is a sociological institution just like every other group of people. Every group of people, including a church, will have norms, procedures, and rules (whether stated or unstated) that guide and govern the interaction of individuals. Because of this, local churches are prone to abuses of power, hypocritical actions, and judgmental attitudes.

But there is nothing that Jesus could build, this side of the new heavens and earth, that wouldn't be this way if it included humans. Every government, every business, every gathering of friends, every book club, every kindergarten class, and every ski team will exhibit institutional weaknesses and failings. But the greatness of the local church is that it is designed to be more than just a human institution. It is designed to be the place where the invisible church is visibly present. It is designed to be the fellowship of the Spirit. Just as we as Christians are empowered to move beyond our human failings through the Holy Spirit, so too the church is able to move beyond its human failings through the power of the Holy Spirit. No other gathering of humans can say that in the same way.

To become a follower of Christ is not to abandon institutions any more than it is to abandon physical bodies. Tom Wright has recently reminded us that salvation is not some disembodied experience of the "spiritual" over against the physical.[63] The same is true of church. To think that church is some deinstitutionalized experience is to play the "spiritual" over against the social. We do not cease being physical when we become Christians. Likewise we do not cease being social when we become Christians. God created us as social beings, and the new heavens and the new earth are going to be social.

The church must not be overly institutional, but it will always be an institution. The difference is that it is designed to be God's institution.

NOTES

1. Mason is a composite person based on those described by George Barna in his book *Revolution* (Carol Stream, IL: Tyndale, 2005).
2. David F. Wells, *The Courage to Be Protestant* (Grand Rapids: Eerdmans, 2008), 179–80.
3. Mimi Greenwood Knight, "Holy Headscratchers," *Christian Parenting Today* (Spring 2003), 29.
4. Martin Luther, "Sermon for Easter Day, 1531," cited by John Webster, *Holiness* (London: SCM, 2003), 73.
5. We should note that there are some reasonable, though incomplete, explanations for the failure of the church. These include the following: (1) Church has not so much been tried and found wanting as it has been found difficult and left untried. Certainly, not every group of people that *calls* itself a church is actually a church. (2) All local churches have people in them who are not actually Christians, and many of the worst evils have been perpetrated by these "wolves in sheep's clothing." (3) We also need to recognize that not every perceived failure of the church is, in fact, a failure. As I've gotten older, I've discovered that my parents were a bit wiser than I thought they were when I was a teenager. In the same way, I find that many of the church's "weaknesses" are actually strengths when you see them with the right perspective. To give a quick example, I always thought that the church wasted a lot of time, but I've learned that God has actually designed his church so that some time is "wasted" (see Marva Dawn, *A Royal "Waste" of Time: The Splendor of Worshiping God and Being Church for the World* (Grand Rapids: Eerdmans, 1999).
6. Alternatively, we could address the question: How does the church bring God glory?—and some of that will show up in these pages—but as John Piper in *Desiring God* has reminded us, enjoying the benefits and blessings of God *is* the way in which God is most glorified. John Piper, *Desiring God: Meditations of a Christian Hedonist* (Sisters, OR: Multnomah, 1996).
7. Andy Argyrakis, "The Prodigal Newsboys," posted October 23, 2006, ChristianMusicToday.com (accessed September 2007).
8. John Stott, *Basic Christianity* (Grand Rapids: Eerdmans, 1954), 128.
9. For example, 96 percent of the time that "church" appears in the NIV it is a direct translation of *ekklesia*.
10. See Ben Campbell Johnson, *GodSpeech: Putting Divine Disclosures into Human Words* (Grand Rapids: Eerdmans, 2006), 98.

11. Bob Spitz, *The Beatles: The Biography* (New York: Little, Brown and Company, 2005), 474–75.

12. This analogy is not perfect because it gives the impression that the more people who are in a church assembly, the better that is, which is not the case. All that is needed, according to Jesus, is two or more.

13. C. S. Lewis, *Surprised by Joy: The Shape of My Early Life* (New York: Harcourt and Brace, 1955), 199–200.

14. J. R. R. Tolkein, *The Lord of the Rings* (Boston: Houghton and Mifflin, 1954).

15. While Paul uses "we" in 1 Cor. 12:13, indicating the universal church, in 12:27 he uses the pronoun "you" and says, "you are the body of Christ," indicating that this idea of the universal church of verse 13 finds its expression in the local church of Corinth.

16. There are actually two exceptions to this rule: physical location and language. Because of the finite nature of humanity in this world and God's actions at the tower of Babel, members of the same local church will reside in the same general geographic area and speak the same language(s).

17. Green Day, "Jesus of Suburbia," accessed at www.metrolyrics.com/jesus-of-suburbia-lyrics-green-day.html (April 20, 2010).

18. David Wells, *The Courage to Be Protestant* (Grand Rapids: Eerdmans, 2008), 158.

19. The Doors, "L.A. Woman."

20. Jacques Ellul, *The Meaning of the City* (Grand Rapids: Eerdmans, 1993), 23.

21. As cited in George Pattison, *Thinking about God in an Age of Technology* (Oxford: Oxford University Press, 2005), 251.

22. Quentin Schultze, *Habits of the Hi-Tech Heart* (Grand Rapids: Baker, 2002), 23.

23. For an explanation of why *koinonia* refers to the local church in 1 Cor 1:9, see J. Samra, *Being Conformed to Christ in Community* (Edinburgh: T&T Clark, 2006), 137–39.

24. Christine Pohl, *Making Room: Recovering Hospitality as a Christian Tradition* (Grand Rapids: Eerdmans, 1999), 12.

25. Amy Dickinson, *The Mighty Queens of Freeville* (New York: Hyperion, 2009), 96.

26. E. R. Dodds, *Pagan and Christian in an Age of Anxiety* (Cambridge: Cambridge University Press, 1965), 136–38.

27. P. D. Eastman, *Are You My Mother?* (New York: Random House, 1960).

28. Cyprian, *The Unity of the Church* 6.

29. Augustine, *Sermons* 216.7.7, cited by *Augustine through the Ages: An Encyclopedia*, ed. Allan Fitzgerald (Grand Rapids: Eerdmans, 1999), 174.

30. For other examples see Tertullian, *De Oratione* 2.6; Clement of Alexandria, *Paedagogus* 1.6, Cyril, *Catechetical Lectures* 18.26.

31. Martin Luther, *Larger Catechism* 3, trans. by Bente and Dau, published in *Triglot Concordia: The Symbolical Books of the Evangelical Lutheran Church* (St. Louis: Concordia, 1921).

32. John Calvin, *Institutes of the Christian Religion* 4.1.1 (trans. H. Beveridge [Peabody, MA: Hendrickson, 2008], 672).

33. For the consensus today see Robert Yarborough, *1 – 3 John* (Grand Rapids: Baker, 2008), 333 – 34; for examples from the early church see Henri de Lubac, *The Motherhood of the Church* (San Francisco: Ignatius Press, 1982), 46.

34. For a discussion of this in relation to Paul's ministry, see J. G. Samra, *Being Conformed to Christ in Community* (Edinburgh: T&T Clark, 2006), 51 – 52.

35. Much of this material comes from Samra, *Being Conformed to Christ.*

36. Wendell, Barry, *Jayber Crow* (New York: Counterpoint, 2000), 30 – 31.

37. James McBride, *The Color of Water: A Black Man's Tribute to His White Mother* (New York: Penguin, 1996).

38. See Kevin Durkin, *Developmental Social Psychology: From Infancy to Old Age* (Oxford: Blackwell, 1995), 487 – 88.

39. This is the alternative reading in the NIV and in my opinion, the more correct reading.

40. Berry, *Jayber Crow*, 38.

41. Roger Gehring, *House Church and Mission* (Peabody, MA: Hendrickson, 2004), 139.

42. Even many in the secular community seem to recognize that it takes more than just a nuclear family to raise a child. Hillary Rodham Clinton wrote a book famously titled, *It Takes a Village* (New York: Simon and Schuster, 1996). The message of her book was that it takes more than an individual parent or even a family to raise a child properly — it takes a larger community. For those who belong to God, that larger community is not just a "village" of neighbors; it is the church of Jesus Christ! *It Takes a Church* could be another title for the New Testament, since the overall message of the Gospels and letters of the New Testament writers focuses on the establishment of a new community of people for the purpose of fulfilling the mission of God.

43. See, for example, Ignatius (died around AD 110), who wrote: "I know that the bishop [of the church of God at Philadelphia] obtained a ministry (which is for the whole community) not by his own efforts nor through men nor out of vanity, but in the love of God the Father and the Lord Jesus Christ … therefore as children of the light of truth flee from division and false teaching. Where the pastor/shepherd is, there follow like sheep." Ignatius, *Letter to the Philadelphians*, 1:1; 2:1, in *The Apostolic Fathers: Greek Texts and English Translations of Their Writings*, 2nd ed., trans. by J. B. Lightfoot, J. R. Harmer, and Michael Holmes (Grand Rapids: Baker, 1992), 176 – 79.

44. Cited in William H. Willimon, *Pastor: A Reader for Ordained Ministry* (Nashville: Abingdon, 2002), 15.

45. Timothy Laniak, *Shepherds after My Own Heart: Pastoral Traditions and Leadership in the Bible*, New Studies in Biblical Theology, ed. D. A. Carson (Downers Grove, IL: InterVarsity Press, 2006), 248.

46. Eugene Peterson, *Under the Unpredictable Plant: An Exploration in Vocational Holiness* (Grand Rapids: Eerdmans, 1992), 180 – 81.

47. Amyotrophic lateral sclerosis, also known as Lou Gehrig's disease.

48. Philip Yancey talks about Ed Dobson and his love for people in his book, *What's So Amazing about Grace?* (Grand Rapids: Zondervan, 1997), 169.

49. God is so passionately concerned with raising up leaders of the highest character for the church that anyone who chooses unqualified people to lead will be held guilty of the sins of those leaders (1 Tim. 5:22)! For this interpretation of 1 Timothy 5:22, see Philip H. Towner, *The Letters to Timothy and Titus*, New International Commentary on the New Testament (Grand Rapids: Eerdmans, 2006), 374–75.

50. "State Sen. Ernie Chambers Sues God: Chambers Aims to Make Point about Frivolous Lawsuits," posted September 17, 2007, www.ketv.com/news/14133442/detail.html (accessed November 20, 2008).

51. Although it says "grace and truth," grace is the more prominent word. Note that in 1:16 John writes (lit.): "from the fullness of his grace we have all received grace upon grace."

52. Karl Barth, *Church Dogmatics*, Vol. IV.1: *The Doctrine of Reconciliation*, ed. G. W. Bromiley and T. F. Torrance, trans. G. W. Bromiley (Edinburgh: T&T Clark, 1956), 661.

53. It is true that Paul wasn't at Antioch when Barnabas arrived, but the grace of God was evident in the Jews and Gentiles worshiping God there.

54. Justin Martyr, *First Apology, Ante-Nicene Fathers*, Volume 1: *The Apostolic Fathers, Justin Martyr, Irenaeus*, ed. Alexander Roberts and James Donaldson (Peabody, MA: Hendrickson, repr. 2004), 67.

55. Tertullian, *Apology* 39; Lucian, *Peregrinus* 13; Julian, *Epistle 22*. These references are from Frances Young, "Christian Attitudes to Finance in the First Four Centuries," *Epworth Review* 4/3 (September 1977): 78–86.

56. David Kinnaman and Gabe Lyons, *unChristian: What a New Generation Really Thinks about Christianity and Why It Matters* (Grand Rapids: Baker, 2007), 242.

57. Brian Sanders, *Life after Church* (Downers Grove, IL: InterVarsity Press, 2007), 178.

58. *Shepherd of Hermas*, from *The Apostolic Fathers*, ed. and trans. Lightfoot, Harmer, and Holmes (Grand Rapids: Baker, 1989), 189–290.

59. Johnny Cash, *Man in Black* (Grand Rapids: Zondervan, 1975), 209.

60. Dietrich Bonhoeffer, *Life Together* (New York: Harper & Row, 1954), 29–30.

61. This section draws on the work of Miroslav Volf, *After Our Likeness: The Church as the Image of the Trinity* (Grand Rapids: Eerdmans, 1998).

62. Whether this legend is true or not is difficult to determine, but it is widely available on the Internet. See, for example, www.ravenhill.org/whitefield.htm.

63. N. T. Wright, *Surprised by Hope* (New York: HarperOne, 2008).